**CHILDREN AND ADULTS WITH
ATTENTION-DEFICIT/HYPERACTIVITY DISORDER**

CHADD Introduction

When the topic of driving by teenagers with attention deficit/hyperactivity disorder has been presented at Annual Conferences sponsored by CHADD Inc. (Children and Adults with Attention Deficit Disorders), parental response has been consistently strong. Therefore, CHADD decided to draw on the expertise of Marlene Snyder, Ph.D., in creating this comprehensive manual, a roadmap for parents of children with AD/HD (and co-occurring disorders) who will soon be learning how to drive.

This manual will prove invaluable in promoting every aspect of safe driving behavior in teens particularly at risk when behind the wheel of a vehicle. Readers will receive an overview of special problems and challenges faced by the young driver, consideration of AD/HD medication issues, a discussion of driver education materials, detailed review of teen driver contracts and incentive programs, a checklist of insurance and state regulations, and much more. The sensitive area of alcohol and substance abuse is also discussed.

In addition, the guide includes practical lists, illustrations, and action items titled "Parent and Teen Activity" with references and suggestions for appropriate follow-up. Perhaps most importantly, adults will recognize and appreciate the important role they play in serving as a positive driving role model and an informed, patient and safe driving teacher to their teen.

CHADD is grateful for the in-depth work and research of Dr. Snyder, who has extensive experience in the education, juvenile justice and parent education fields. The input on the project of Rae Hemphill, a member of the CHADD National Board of Directors and former coordinator of the CHADD chapter in Northern Virginia, is also appreciated.

The production and distribution of this special edition was made possible by grants from Eli Lilly and Company and State Farm Insurance. CHADD wishes to acknowledge and thank them for their generous financial backing of this guide and commitment to its development.

CHADD is the leading national, nonprofit, tax-exempt IRS 501 (c)(3) organization working to improve the lives of people affected by attention deficit/hyperactivity disorder. For further information contact CHADD, 8181 Professional Place – Suite 201, Landover, MD 20785, telephone (301) 306-7070, website www.chadd.org

Mission Statement

CHADD works to improve the lives of people affected by AD/HD through:

- **C**ollaborative Leadership
- **A**dvocacy
- **R**esearch
- **E**ducation
- **S**upport

CHADD®

CHILDREN AND ADULTS WITH
ATTENTION-DEFICIT/
HYPERACTIVITY DISORDER

CHADD CARES!

AD/HD
& Driving

A Guide for Parents of Teens with AD/HD

J. Marlene Snyder, Ph.D.

Whitefish Consultants
P.O. Box 1744
Whitefish, MT 59937
www.whitefishconsultants.com

Whitefish Consultants
P.O. Box 1744
Whitefish, Montana 59937
www.whitefishconsultants.com

ISBN   0-9708813-0-4

Library of Congress Control Number: 2001116685

Cover Design and Printing by American Printing
75 First Avenue W.N., Kalispell, MT 59901

Cover Photograph by Chuck Jackson© 2001

Printed in the United States of America

Acknowledgments

As a book is written and published, a number of highly supportive people become involved. The acknowledgments page is like a curtain call, where those talented associates can step forward, receive thanks, and take a bow.

My son, Kevin, continues to be one of the most important teachers in my life. His energy, enthusiasm for life, and safe driving techniques always amaze me. Our love for Kevin as parents inspired me to write this book.

Lee Snyder, M.S., M.P.A., R.S., C.C., and M.H.B.F. (my husband and best friend), has always supported any project that I undertake. Without his willingness to read, listen, discuss, and support every aspect of this project, I would not have made the trip to the printer!

Special thanks to Sam Goldstein, Ph.D., Gerald Rouse, J.D., Gayle Weinberg, Ph.D., Kevin Murphy, Ph.D., Mark Katz, Ph.D., Pam Hughes, M.A., Craig Walker, Ph.D., Bruce Steadman, LCSW, David Turner, M.S., Rae Hemphill, Geoff Kewley, M.D., Dana McMurray and Stephanie Rouse. They are most encouraging, kind, and patient friends.

Martin Barry, Art Instructor, and the talented guys at Mountain High School, Kaysville, Utah, provided many illustrations. Thanks to Adam McCafferty, Isiah Amborsini, Matt Lorenzen, Vincente Utrera, and James Pinko. One special young lady, Harley Addison, contributed several illustrations. Spencer Hughes and Kate Jordan are the good-looking teens in the cover photo.

Thanks to the entire team at American Printing, especially Phil and Connie Bartlett, Moe Zimmerman, and Jodi Walker for their professionalism, encouragement, customer service, and upbeat, "can do" attitude!

And finally, to those parents and teens who shared their personal stories goes great respect and gratitude. Through the harsh reality of your experiences, readers will more clearly hear the message of this work.

AD/HD & Driving

A Guide for Parents of Teens with AD/HD

Illustration by Adam McCafferty

Table of Contents

Preface

Why is this manual important for you and your teen?

All parents of teens who drive experience the challenge of educating and training their adolescents to be safe, responsible drivers. Parents of teens with AD/HD or other behavioral disorders may find this task even more challenging. This manual was written especially for parents of teens with AD/HD and coexisting disorders. The purpose of this book is to help parents promote safe driving behaviors and to minimize the risks associated with learning to drive. Throughout the five chapters of this book, parent and teen activities are suggested to help achieve this purpose. Teaching a teen to drive can be an opportunity for parent and teen to spend time together and develop a stronger parent-child relationship. Parents should skim the entire book and select important issues for family discussion and rule making *before* the teen is given the opportunity to learn how to drive.

Chapter 1: An overview of teen driving research is provided. The research demonstrates the overwhelming need for parents to take action to reduce the risks associated with teen driving. Increased risks associated with teens who have AD/HD or coexisting disorders will also be discussed.

Chapter 2: The second chapter identifies characteristic behaviors for individuals with AD/HD and other coexisting disorders. Resources are suggested that provide information as to how these disorders can be treated.

Chapter 3: General tips are provided for parents whose teens exhibit difficult behaviors. This chapter stresses the importance of setting clear rules and consistent consequences.

Chapter 4: This chapter identifies 20 steps that parents can use as a guide in the process of helping their teenagers to become safe drivers. The first ten steps should be completed before the child is allowed to apply for a learner's permit.

Chapter 5: The final chapter presents strategies for dealing with teens who are not able to handle their driving privileges responsibly.

NOTE TO THE READER:

• For reader convenience, the term AD/HD is used to note Attention Deficit/Hyperactivity Disorder generally and does not differentiate between AD/HD, Hyperactive Impulsive Type; AD/HD, Predominately Inattentive Type (ADD - without hyperactivity); and AD/HD, Combined Type.

• In order to avoid gender bias and the awkward and distracting use of such combination forms as he/she or (s)he, the author uses gender neutral terms. This is done in an effort to help readers recognize AD/HD is a condition that causes problems for males and females alike.

• Resources are provided as a service to readers and no product, service, or organization is being promoted or endorsed. It is the responsibility of readers to make their own inquiries and their own decisions as to the usefulness of these resources.

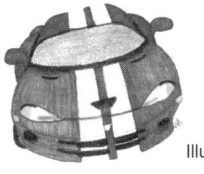

Introduction

Today's parents are often overwhelmed by time commitments and caretaking tasks that come with raising a busy family. Parents may look forward to having another driver in the family who can help run errands and drive a younger sister or brother to their soccer practice and piano lessons. The thought of a teenager being able to drive to school, to extra-curricular activities, to the dentist, to a friend's home, to the mall, and to the movies has great appeal!

For teenagers, driving enhances their status within the family. It's an experience that is greatly anticipated and creates excitement in their lives and in the lives of their peers. It's a part of growing up that will always be remembered. Think for a moment about the first time that you got behind the wheel! Driving is such an important step in gaining recognition as an adult that most people remember their first driving experience vividly.

I grew up on a farm near Liberty, Nebraska, where farm families had their own "graduated licensing" programs. Children started driving tractors for hay crews before we were out of first grade! I remember having to stand up on the clutch of the old John Deere "B" with both feet to disengage it so that I could pound the shifter in gear. Young drivers quickly graduated from "granny gear" in the hay fields to "road gear" on graveled country roads, and from driving straight ahead to learning how to drive in reverse. As an elementary student you graduated from driving the tractor to driving the riding lawn mower; then to the pickup truck to deliver meals to the fields; and finally, to the large farm truck to haul harvest grains. When rural teens were 14, they drove the family car alone to school. By the time they enrolled in the school's driver education classes, they'd already driven thousands of miles!

The way I learned to drive was far removed from the situation that our son experienced. We no longer lived on the farm. Instead, we lived in a community of 12,000 souls, a maze of busy streets, and a four-lane highway. Before getting his learner's permit, our son's driving experience had been limited to pedal-powered hot wheels, bicycles, golf carts, and riding lawn mowers.

At the time we taught our son how to drive, my husband and I did not fully appreciate the impact of AD/HD on an individual's driving ability. We were also naive as to the level of parental support and involvement that would be needed to provide enough supervised practice for our son to learn safe driving behaviors. During our son's high school years, several of his schoolmates were killed in motor vehicle accidents. Attending funerals of teenage friends, and extending sympathy to their parents, made us approach much more cautiously the very real dangers facing teen drivers.

Real life experiences and safety concerns kept our son driving on a learner's permit well beyond his sixteenth birthday! Even with all the extra vigilance, coaching, and monitoring, we have experienced our share of driving-related troubles.

At the CHADD National Conference in 1997 Dr. Russell Barkley presented his outcome study on young adults with AD/HD. His report was a wake up call for parents of children with AD/HD. I became interested in using emerging research findings on drivers with AD/HD to develop some driving guidelines for parents of teens with AD/HD. With Dr. Russell Barkley's and Dr. Kevin Murphy's early guidance and encouragement, Rae Hemphill and I conducted the first workshop on AD/HD and Teen Drivers in 1998. That presentation, with four pages of handout materials and a teen driver contract, sparked CHADD National's interest in producing a pamphlet to alert members to the important issues involved in preparing teens with AD/HD to become safe drivers. The idea grew into this guidebook for parents.

Over the years, we have all heard story after story about "accidents" caused by poor judgment, impulsiveness, lack of driving experience, inattentiveness, and bad attitude. Each one of our children's unintentional "accidents" could have ended in a fatal automobile crash. So often we hear, "Well, it was just an accident." Used in that context, the word "accident" has taken on a benign, excusable connotation, and it does not convey the impact and tragedy common to automobile crashes. I have chosen to use the term "accident" throughout the book, because these situations are unintentional and are caused by inexperience. When you see the word "accident" used in this book, however, please remember that an "accident" often reflects a violent, painful, life-altering injury, or even a fatal reality.

Never forget that wonderful teenagers, sons and daughters, with or without AD/HD, die by the thousands in automobile accidents on America's highways every year. It is critical that we all consider thoughtfully how we can more effectively teach our children to become safe drivers.

"Words are things and a small drop of ink.
Falling like dew upon a thought, produces that
which makes thousands, perhaps millions, think."
-Byron

I sincerely hope that you, as parents of teens with AD/HD, will read these words and many other words taken from new research about effective treatments for AD/HD and coexisting conditions. Read, think, and then act to protect your children.

Marlene Snyder, Ph.D.

PROCEED WITH CAUTION

Chapter 1

An Overview of Teen Driving Statistics and Research on Teen Drivers with AD/HD

Highway motor vehicle collisions are the biggest killer of adolescents in this country. Your teenager is more likely to suffer a serious injury or even death from a motor vehicle collision than from diseases, drug overdoses, homicides, and suicides. According to the National Highway Traffic Safety Administration (NHTSA), 5,749 people between the ages of 15 and 20 died in motor vehicle accidents in 1999. Although teens constitute only 7% of licensed American drivers, they account for 14% of drivers involved in fatal collisions. The fatality rate for teenage drivers, based on estimated annual travel, is about four times higher than the death rate for drivers 25 to 69 years old. An additional 348,000 teenagers were injured, some maimed or disabled for life, in motor vehicle accidents.

Experts in the field of highway traffic safety at NHTSA estimate that approximately one out of four teenagers will be involved in a traffic accident during their teen years, and one out of twenty teens will be involved in a serious injury or fatal car accident. The financial costs of property damages in teen driver accidents each year are estimated to be well over $31 billion. These costs do not include medical costs, burial costs, long-term medical care, or the lifelong emotional costs for the families experiencing the death or serious injury of their family members.

First-Year Drivers and Their Passengers
Are at Greatest Risk!

National driving statistics from the Insurance Institute for Highway Safety consistently show that the first years of driving are the most dangerous (Table 1). Sixteen-year-olds are more likely to speed, less likely to wear a seat belt, and are 12 times more likely to die in a car accident than any other age group. Three times as many 16-year-old drivers die in motor vehicle accidents than do 17-year-old drivers. Higher proportions of 16-year-olds are responsible for their own fatal accidents compared with other drivers. Police reports show that over a third of all 16-year-old drivers in fatal accidents were speeding, or, if they were not exceeding the limit, they were going too fast for road conditions. Approximately two-thirds of the teens who died as passengers were in vehicles driven by other teens. Death statistics for teen drivers also show that most teen fatalities occur in rural rather than urban areas.

Table 1

Percentage of Fatal Crashes by Characteristic, 1998.
Source: Insurance Institute for Highway Safety.

Fatal Crashes	Driver's Age		
	16	17-19	20-49
Driver Error	80%	75%	62%
Speeding	36	31	22
Single Vehicle	41	37	30
3+ Occupants	33	26	19
.01 Blood Alcohol	13	32	59
Female Drivers	35	29	30

Parents should keep in mind that all of the statistics mentioned to this point apply to the general population of teenagers in the United States. Unfortunately, research is showing that young drivers with Attention Deficit/Hyperactivity Disorder (AD/HD), or other coexisting disorders with high-risk behaviors, experience even higher risks for serious driving difficulties.

Even Greater Risk Exists for Young Drivers with AD/HD!

Barkley, Murphy, and Kwasnik compared the driving records, skills, and knowledge of 25 young adults with AD/HD (ages 17 to 30), with other young adults of the same age, gender, ethnicity, and educational status. The researchers interviewed the participants about their driving histories and patterns, the number and types of traffic citations they had received, and the number of motor vehicle accidents in which they had been involved. The researchers verified these statistics by checking state driving records. Each participant in the study was then tested using a videotaped test of driving knowledge and a computerized driving simulator. In addition, participants and their parents (or others who knew the participants) were asked about the participants' driving behaviors.

Highlights of the research findings were:

- All of the participants in the AD/HD group reported receiving at least one speeding ticket, a figure nearly twice that for the control group (without AD/HD). In addition, state records revealed that the drivers with AD/HD had more than five times as many traffic citations on their records than did the non-AD/HD control group. Most of the traffic tickets were for speeding or failure to yield.

- Participants with AD/HD were nearly four times more likely than the controls to have been the driver in an accident that resulted in injuries.

- Participants with AD/HD were nearly seven times more likely than the controls to be involved in two or more accidents.

- Participants with AD/HD were over four times more likely than the controls to be at fault for the accidents in which they were involved.

- Reports from participants with AD/HD and reports from their parents or other parties rated the participants with AD/HD as having significantly poorer driving habits than members of the control group.

- Participants with AD/HD were more likely to have had their licenses suspended or revoked, and had a greater number of suspensions or revocations than the controls.

These research findings were supported by similar studies conducted at the University of California at Berkeley (Lambert et, al); the University of Massachusetts Medical Center (Barkley et, al.); and in Canada (Weiss et, al.);

3

and Germany (Beck et, al.). Studies sponsored by the Health Research Council of New Zealand and conducted by Nada-Raja, et, al. involved 916 adolescents between the ages of 15 and 18. This large study reported similar findings to those of the smaller research projects.

Generally, these studies found that the most common driving violations occurring with teens with AD/HD were speeding, failure to obey signs and signals (failure to yield), following too closely (tailgating), improper passing, and failure to follow road markings. In Lambert's study at the University of California at Berkeley, drivers with AD/HD were found more likely to have been cited for reckless driving and drunk driving than drivers without AD/HD. The study conducted in Germany found that teens with AD/HD had significantly higher rates of traffic accident involvement **before** getting their driver's license than teens without AD/HD. The New Zealand study reported that females with AD/HD had significantly more driving offenses and more traffic accidents when compared with females who did not have the disorder.

> *"AD/HD is not a problem of knowing... it's a problem of doing what you know," Russell Barkley, Ph.D.*

In the Barkley, Murphy, and Kwasnik driving study, subjects with AD/HD performed as well as other subjects without AD/HD on the test of driving knowledge. "Knowing what to do, therefore, does not seem to be the problem with drivers having AD/HD," they noted in their report. Rather, it is with the actual performance of driving and the exercising of sound driving habits that drivers with AD/HD seem to have their difficulties. Most teens with AD/HD will be able to recite the rules of the road — but may have trouble applying the rules while they are behind the wheel!

Knowledge and Performance Are Two Different Things

A good driver education course that emphasizes on-the-road driving is an effective way for teens to learn basic theory about vehicle control skills. According to the National Highway Traffic Safety Administration (NHTSA), however, simply educating young drivers about the rules of the road is not effective in reducing accidents among teen drivers. There is no correlation between driver education, either in public schools or in private commercial driving schools, and lower accident rates for teens.

Gaining knowledge of highway rules doesn't improve the teen driver's perception, general driving, or reaction skills. Excellent quiz scores on driving rules do nothing to develop good attitudes or alter the risk-taking or thrill-seeking tendencies associated with immature judgment behind the wheel. Driver education courses cannot be expected to teach all that the teen needs to know in just a few hours of behind-the-wheel training. These skills are gained only through driving practice.

NHTSA traffic safety experts have pointed out that driver education courses may even contribute to high accident rates because teens get a false sense of confidence in themselves and their abilities upon completion of a driver education course. Parents should not assume that their teen will be a safe driver merely because the teenager successfully completed a driver education class, or achieved a perfect score on the knowledge component of a driver's test. An effective driver education program must be integrated with a graduated licensing system and parental guidance and monitoring of the teen's driving behaviors.

Parents of Teens with AD/HD Face Additional Risks

Most parents of teens with AD/HD are not surprised to see evidence of higher driving risks associated with AD/HD. These parents have most likely observed deficiencies in attention, persistence, activity regulation, eye-hand coordination, gross motor control, reaction time, and rule-following behaviors in their children from an early age. Some of these parents have realized that their young children with AD/HD are accident-prone and seem to visit their doctor or hospital more than do children without AD/HD.

Researchers at the Mayo Clinic, led by Cynthia Liebson, Ph.D., found that "Individuals with AD/HD compared with those without AD/HD exhibited a significantly increased likelihood of hospital inpatient, hospital outpatient, and ED (emergency department) admissions." The researchers went on to say, "These findings are consistent with multiple reports that individuals with AD/HD exhibit more psychosocial co-morbidity, chronic health conditions, and adverse medical outcomes (e.g., substance abuse, automobile collisions, and fractures)."

When considering the driver's license, some parents of adolescents with AD/HD may not be aware that they are at an even greater risk than parents of teens without AD/HD for experiencing:

- Serious injury or death of a child in a motor vehicle accident;
- Higher incidence of property damage;
- Higher health care costs;
- More involvement with legal and liability issues; and
- Higher motor vehicle insurance rates.

What Can Parents Do?

At this point, it is important to remind parents that some teenagers who do not have AD/HD have lousy driving records, and many teens with AD/HD have become safe drivers. Teens with AD/HD are not automatically doomed to driving failure. In fact, the difference between unsafe and safe teen drivers with AD/HD may have more to do with their **parents' behavior!** Parents that model safe behaviors and provide a great deal of structure for their teen's beginning driving experience are more likely to have safe teen drivers.

Teens with AD/HD who have had reasonably good driving records, have parents who have been willing to take responsibility for their teens' learning safe driving behaviors. These parents have made teaching driving safety a top priority. Parents of teen drivers with AD/HD spend a great deal of time monitoring their teen's driving behaviors. These parents have spent extra time coaching their teens on the application of highway rules and providing opportunities for their teens to develop safe driving skills, emotional maturity, good judgment, and proper attitudes. These parents are well prepared to provide consistent consequences for inappropriate driving behaviors in order to:

- Protect their teen driver from injury;
- Protect the safety of other community members (drivers, pedestrians, and passengers) who share the streets and highways with the teen driver; and
- Protect themselves from the grief caused by the serious injury or death of a child, the death or injury of another caused by your teen, and related legal involvement due to property loss and liability issues.

It's also important for parents of teens with AD/HD to understand that AD/HD is often complicated by the coexistence of other disorders and their associated high-risk behaviors. Individuals with AD/HD are likely to have other complicating conditions that frequently mask or camouflage the underlying AD/HD symptoms. AD/HD is not just a benign condition that affects only high-energy little boys who will eventually grow out of it. AD/HD is a serious disorder and has major consequences for society as well as for the people who have the disorder. Behaviors associated with these conditions are presented in the following chapter.

References:

Barkley, R., Guevremont, D., Anastopoulos, A., DuPaul, G., and Shelton, T. (1993). Driving-Related Risks and Outcomes of Attention Deficit Hyperactivity Disorder in Adolescents and Young Adults: A 3 to 5-Year Follow-Up Survey. *Pediatrics.* Vol. 2, 212-218.

Barkley, R., Murphy, K., and Kwasnik, D. (1996). Vehicle Driving Competencies and Risks in Teens and Young Adults with Attention Deficit Hyperactivity Disorder. *Pediatrics,* Vol. 98, No.6, 1089-1095.

Beck, N., Warnke, A., Kruger, H., and Barglik, W. (1996). Hyperkinetic Syndrome and Behavioral Disorders in Street Traffic: A Case Control Pilot Study. *Z Kinder Jugendpsychiatr Psychother.* Vol. 24, No. 2, 82-91. (This article is in German.)

Chen, L., Baker, S. P., Braver, E. R., and Guohua, L. (2000). Carrying Passengers as a Risk Factor for Crashes Fatal to 16- and 17-Year-Old Drivers. *Journal of the American Medical Association,* Vol. 283, No. 12.

Insurance Institute for Highway Safety. (2000). Highway Loss Data Institute. Website: www.iihs.org/safety_facts/teens/beginning_drivers.htm

Lambert, N. M., Harsough, C. S., Sassone, S. and Sandoval, J. (1987). Persistence of hyperactive symptoms from childhood to adolescence and associated outcomes. *American Journal of Orthopsychiatry,* Vol. 57, 22-32.

Leibson, C. L., Katusic, S. K., Barbaresi, W. J., Ranson, J., and O'Brien, P. C. (2001). Use and Costs of Medical Care for Children and Adolescents With and Without Attention Deficit/Hyperactivity Disorder. *Journal of the American Medical Association,* Vol 285, No. 1.

Nada-Raja, S., Langley, J., McGee, R., Williams, S., Begg, D. and Reeder, A. (1997). Inattentive and Hyperactive Behaviors and Driving Offenses in Adolescence. *Journal of American Academy Child & Adolescent Psychiatry.* Vol. 36, No. 4, 515-522.

National Center for Statistics and Analysis. (1999). *Traffic Safety Facts 1998 - Young Drivers,* Research Development Department, 400 Seventh Street, S. W., Washington, D.C. 20590.

National Highway Traffic Safety Administration, NHTSA Information, 400 Seventh Street, S.W., Washington, D.C. 20590. Web site: www.nhtsa.dot.govm 1-800-424-9393

Weiss, G. and Hechtman, L. (1993). Hyperactive Children Grown Up. (2nd Ed). New York: Guilford Press.

Chapter 2

Behavioral Characteristics of AD/HD and Coexisting Disorders

In the last decade, scientists have made great progress in learning about attention deficit disorders. New technologies have made it possible to learn about the brain, but scientific understanding of how the brain works is still in the beginning stages. PET scans (positron emission tomography), MRI (magnetic resources imaging), and SPECT scans (single photon emission computed tomography) have provided evidence that AD/HD is a neurobiological condition. As technology advances, researchers will learn more about AD/HD.

Attention Deficit/Hyperactivity Disorder (AD/HD), which includes attention-deficit without hyperactivity, is a neurological condition of the brain. In the AD/HD brain, messages from the outside world do not pass consistently from nerve to nerve. As a result, people with AD/HD take longer to process information and are prone to impulsive reactions.

Doctors have observed behavioral symptoms of AD/HD in children for nearly a century and have conducted an estimated 6,000 studies on the disorder. But only in the past decade has medical technology advanced to the point where researchers are able to actually look at the working brain. Brain scans, coupled with advances in genetics research, have given scientists their first real clues to what is different in the AD/HD brain. Researchers suspect that attention deficit disorder may turn out to have many different forms.

The following four major findings in brain research are just starting points in our understanding of AD/HD. In the future, we will have a better understanding regarding how to help those with AD/HD.

Figures 1, 3, and 4, as well as the text describing these figures, were adapted with permission from "The Inside Story of AD/HD," *Cape Cod Times,* Special Edition, June 2, 1998.

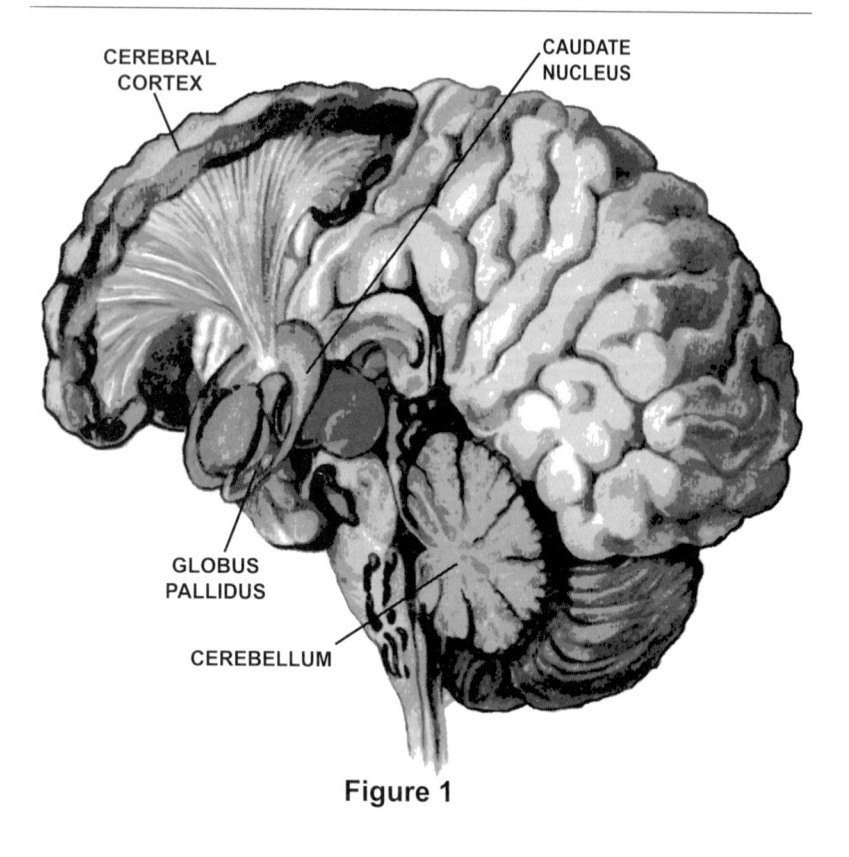

Figure 1

1. **Smaller right brain.** The brain has two hemispheres, with the right side usually larger than the left. Using Magnetic Resonance Imaging, scientists have shown that the right hemisphere is an average of 5.2% smaller in individuals with AD/HD compared to individuals who do not have the condition. The AD/HD brain appears to be symmetrical. Three structures; the cerebellum, caudate nucleus, and globus pallidus are smaller in the right side of the brain in individuals with AD/HD.

The brain's command center is located just behind the forehead and in the pre-frontal cerebral cortex. It is responsible for impulse control and physical movement. While the initiation of movement is felt to lie in the pre-frontal region of the cortex, the coordinated expression of movement is controlled by the cerebellum which lies atop the brainstem.

The caudate nucleus and globus pallidus are near the middle of the brain and translate commands into action. These are the exact areas of the brain that are known to be responsible for executive functions such as planning and time management.

2. **Underactivity in the brain.** AD/HD adults burn sugar more slowly in the frontal lobes of the brain. This results in less energy and less activity in areas of the brain linked to attention span and motor control. It isn't that these people with AD/HD have too much or too little sugar in their systems. The problem is that attention-deficit adults are not metabolizing or burning sugar fast enough, so they can't power up the functions in that area of the brain. To demonstrate this metabolic difference, researchers asked people to push a buzzer every time they heard a particular tone. This task was chosen because it required the participant to use a part of the brain that earlier studies had shown to be activated when a person was asked to pay attention. While the exam was going on, scientists used technology called a PET scan–positron emission tomography–that activates a color monitor as sugar is burned in the brain and converted to brain activity (Figure 2). Cerebral blood flow is reduced in some parts, near the front of the brain, that control attention, impulsivity (the ability to "stop and think" before acting), and sensitivity to rewards and punishment.

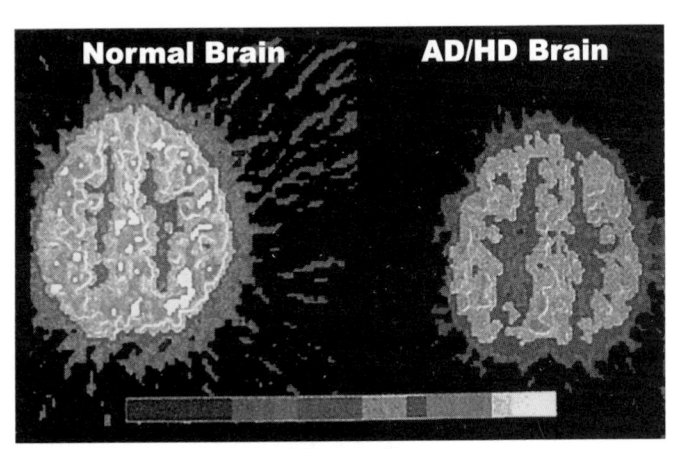

Figure 2

Figure 2. Representative Transverse Images (Left, Normal Control; Right, Patient with Attention Deficit Disorder with Hyperactivity). The two subjects were selected as representative of the hyperactive and control groups. The white and lighter areas indicate areas of relatively high glucose metabolism, whereas the darker areas indicate areas of lower glucose metabolism.

3. **Inefficient connections.** Messages move through our brains as a series of electrical impulses, traveling from one nerve ending, across a synapse, to another nerve ending. Dopamine is the brain chemical, or neurotransmitter, that carries the impulses (Figure 3).

Protein on the outside of the cells literally catches the message-carrying dopamine, traveling in G-protein sacs. The more dopamine that is captured by the cell, the clearer is the message. There are five genes responsible for making the protein that catches dopamine.

Recently, separate studies have confirmed that the dopamine-4 receptor gene (DRD4) is unusually configured in people with AD/HD. Researchers think the defect may result in a protein that's too long to catch well. The finding is exciting because it has been repeated by different laboratories with the same results. Two other studies have shown that people who have a propensity for thrill seeking and other behaviors common to AD/HD also have the unusual DRD4 receptor.

A genetic abnormality in the dopamine receptors (DRD2 and DRD4) and a dopamine transporter gene (DAT1), prevent the structure from efficiently catching the brain chemical dopamine, needed to carry messages across the gap from one nerve ending to another. This situation can explain lapses in an individual's attention, missed information, or difficulty in regulating behavior. Medication helps brain cells make the connection more efficiently.

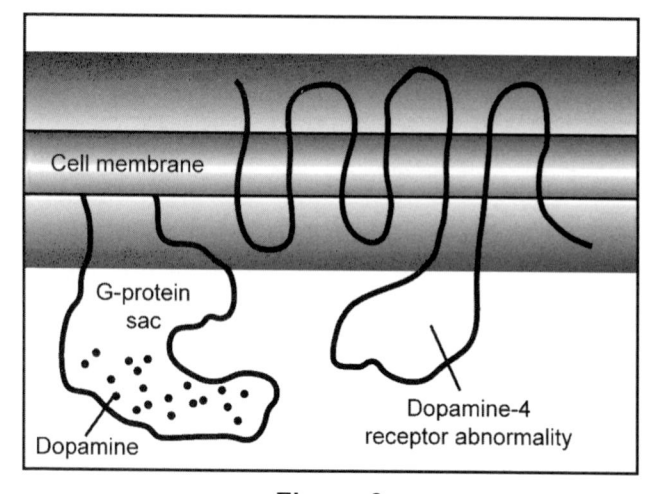

Figure 3

4. **Stimulant medications** appear to work by keeping the message-carrying dopamine in the synaptic gap longer, allowing the message to continue on its way. The longer dopamine is in the gap, the stronger the circuit on which the message travels and the better the chance of "connecting" (Figure 4).

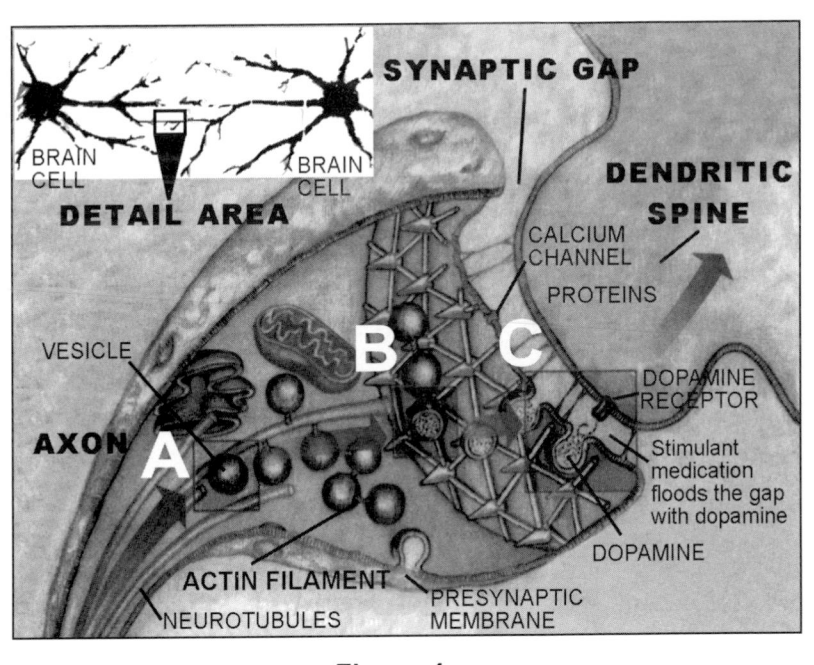

Figure 4

A. **Vesicle balls** carrying dopamine (a neurotransmitter) ride up on the brain cells' neurotubes.

B. **A chemical** process cuts the actin filament holding the balls to the neurotubules. The balls dissolve into the membrane.

C. **The dopamine** is released, and binds to the receptor, forming a bridge. The message, as an electrical pulse (arrows), can then cross the bridge to the other brain cell (dendritic spine) and complete the circuit .

The AD/HD Diagnosis

The characteristic behaviors that define the condition of AD/HD are found in varying degrees in all human beings. To receive a diagnosis of AD/HD, however, these characteristics must be so prevalent in the individual that they impair the individual's ability to handle expected day-to-day functioning in an age-appropriate manner. Keep in mind that your child may not display all the characteristics of AD/HD listed here. In addition, you should know that three identified subtypes of AD/HD have been outlined in the Diagnostic and Statistical Manual, 4th Edition (DSM-IV, pp. 83-85). These are:

1. AD/HD - Predominantly Hyperactive, Impulsive Type;
2. AD/HD - Predominantly Inattentive Type (without hyperactivity); and
3. AD/HD - Combined Type. Diagnostic behaviors are set out in three categories within the DSM-IV: inattentiveness, hyperactivity, and impulsivity.

Inattention Characteristics

- Often fails to give close attention to details or makes careless mistakes in schoolwork, work, or other activities
- Often has difficulty sustaining attention in tasks
- Often does not seem to listen when spoken to directly
- Often does not follow through on instructions and fails to finish school-work, chores, or duties in the workplace (not due to oppositional behavior or failure to understand instructions)
- Often has difficulty organizing tasks and activities
- Often avoids, dislikes, or is reluctant to engage in tasks that require sustained mental effort (such as schoolwork or homework)
- Often loses things necessary for tasks or activities (e.g., toys, school assignments, pencils, books, tools, or keys)
- Is often distracted by extraneous stimuli
- Is often forgetful in daily activities

Hyperactivity Characteristics

- Often fidgets with hands or feet or squirms in seat
- Often leaves seat in classroom or in other situations in which remaining seated is expected

- Often runs about or climbs excessively in situations in which it is inappropriate (in adolescents or adults, may be limited to subjective feelings of restlessness)
- Often has difficulty playing or engaging in leisure activities quietly
- Is often "on the go" or often acts as if "driven by a motor"
- Often talks excessively

Impulsivity Characteristics

- Often blurts out answers before the questions have been completed
- Often has difficulty awaiting turn
- Often interrupts or intrudes on others (e.g., butts into conversations or games)

Even though the characteristics of impulsivity make up the shortest list in the formal diagnostic criteria, not being able to inhibit behaviors long enough to think them through first may present the most severe problems for beginning drivers. This is the characteristic behavior often described by parents as "leaping before looking," "doing before thinking," or "firing before aiming."

Teenagers with AD/HD

One of the many myths surrounding AD/HD is that it is outgrown by the teenage years. This is far from the truth! Although the symptom most obvious to the casual observer–hyperactivity–has often declined by puberty, the other core symptoms remain in the majority of individuals with AD/HD. Impulsiveness can still present a very significant problem. While physical impulsiveness and hyperactivity has often lessened by puberty, adolescents with AD/HD are likely to be much more verbally and emotionally impulsive. They interrupt conversations, speak out of turn, and lose friendships because of inappropriate remarks. They may explode into frequent tantrums, and often seem immune to rational and reasoned argument. Their difficulty with rule-governed behavior means that they may try to push the limits, argue, have difficulties with behavior at school, and are frequently excluded. Inattentiveness also remains in adolescents, and is especially prevalent in girls with AD/HD.

There is a wide range of behavior patterns shown by teenagers (boys and girls) with AD/HD. At one extreme, there are those who are conduct-disordered and at extremely high risk for behaviors that put them at odds with law enforcement. There are others who have good social skills, thrive on a great deal of stimulation, and may be the life of the party with reasonable (although superficial) personal relationships. Some teens with AD/HD are very intelligent, but have underachieved academically, have low self-esteem and poor social skills. These teens may be anxious, depressed, or obsessive. It is important that parents consider the full impact of AD/HD and address the condition with appropriate treatment.

At the present time, effective treatments for AD/HD include: parent education; behavior management techniques; individual and family counseling; educational interventions; and when necessary, medication. New studies point to the importance of using medication to improve the effectiveness of other interventions.

Illustration by Adam McCafferty

Untreated AD/HD

According to the 1998 National Institute of Health (NIH) Consensus Statement on the Diagnosis and Treatment of AD/HD, "Children with AD/HD have pronounced impairments and can experience long-term adverse effects on academic performance, vocational success, and social-emotional development which have a profound impact on individuals, families, schools and society." Recent studies show that children who receive adequate treatment for AD/HD have fewer problems with school, peers, family relationships, and substance abuse, and show improved overall function, compared to those who do not receive treatment. Figure 5 represents some of the developments associated with untreated AD/HD over time.

If your teen has been diagnosed with AD/HD and you are not well versed in the ways that AD/HD impacts behavior, or the proven multi-modal treatments for AD/HD, your teen will be well served by your learning all you can about the condition of AD/HD. A list of excellent resources for information about teenagers with AD/HD is found at the end of this chapter. Treatment for AD/HD should be well underway before your teen is allowed to get a learner's permit.

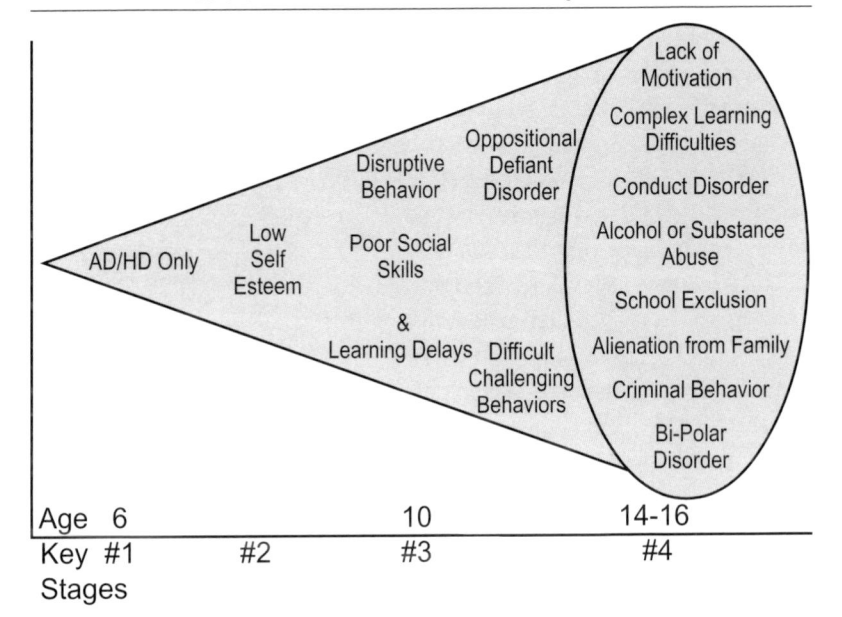

Age 6   10   14-16
Key #1   #2   #3   #4
Stages

Figure 5. Unmanaged, AD/HD can give rise to increasing complications.

Adapted and printed with permission from: *Attention Deficit Hyperactivity Disorder: Recognition, Reality and Resolution,* by Dr. G. D. Kewley, LAC Press, 2nd Floor; 44 Springfield Road, Horsham, W. Sussex, RH12 2PD, United Kingdom.

Coexisting Disorders

Youth with diagnosed AD/HD often have coexisting conditions with separate characteristic behaviors that present additional challenges to young drivers. Coexisting Disorders are described in the DSM-IV as "comorbid conditions". Years ago, it was thought that individuals either had AD/HD *or* Conduct Disorder *or* Anxiety Disorder. It has been learned that individuals may in fact have both AD/HD *and* another disorder. Most studies suggest that approximately 60-70% of all youth with AD/HD have at least one other coexisting condition that will complicate their treatment. It is estimated that between 25% and 35% of youth with AD/HD also have a specific learning disability. Oppositional Defiant Disorder (ODD) is found in 40% to 59% of youth with AD/HD. Between 14% and 43% of adolescents with AD/HD will also have the more serious behavior problems of Conduct Disorder, while 34% to 37% will have some sort of anxiety disorder. Substance abuse problems occur in only 5% of those with AD/HD. That rate escalates to between 40% and 52% when AD/HD coexists with Conduct Disorder.

Many of these disorders have symptoms that ovelap with those of

AD/HD and can confuse and complicate both diagnosis and treatment. Accurate diagnosis of the presence and degree of impairment caused by coexisting conditions is essential for successful treatment of both AD/HD and the coexisting disorder. To further complicate this picture, adolescents with AD/HD will have very different overall symptoms depending not only on their core AD/HD symptoms and coexisting complications, but behaviors will also be influenced by their IQ, family environment, peer relationships, and their adolescent developmental stage.

AD/HD and each of the coexisting disorders must be recognized and considered carefully as to how they impact the teen's skills and behaviors related to driving. It must be determined whether these behaviors can be managed in order to help the teen develop the skills required to be a safe driver. Parents need to work closely with their teen, physician, and mental health professionals to make thoughtful and well-reasoned treatment decisions.

The following information concerns "coexisting conditions" or disorders that are likely to occur with AD/HD. Full diagnostic criteria for these disorders are found in the American Psychiatric Association's Diagnostic and Statistical Manual of Mental Disorders (DSM-IV). This information is presented solely for the purpose of describing the kinds of behaviors that parents of teens with AD/HD may encounter.

Characteristics Associated with Learning Disabilities

Learning disabilities are disorders of one or more basic psychological processes involved in understanding and using written or spoken language that result in an impaired ability to listen, think, speak, read, spell, or do mathematical calculations. Specific learning disabilities include dyslexia, dysgraphia, dyscalculia, and perceptual disorders. Individuals with learning disabilities often exhibit one or more of the following characteristics discussed in the DSM-IV, pp. 48-55:

- Difficulties with translating oral language into information, resulting in inappropriate or contradictory responses to instructions, questions, and persons in authority
- Poorly developed social skills, which result in a lack of understanding of social cues, giving the impression of being discourteous and headstrong
- Difficulty with spatial relationships (could experience problems of depth perception or confusion between right and left hand)
- Poor impulse control
- Poor choices in peer relationships

- Risk-taking behaviors

If specific learning disabilities are found, special education services are available to help your child with their difficulties. An Individual Education Plan should be implemented at your school. Parents need to give school officials permission to start the process of testing for specific learning disabilities or other problems that may impact learning. Learning disabilities can complicate reading signs or understanding directions when learning to drive.

Characteristics Associated with Disruptive Behavior Disorders

Oppositional Defiant Disorder (ODD) is expressed as a recurrent pattern of negative, defiant, disobedient, and hostile behaviors toward authority figures. Those behaviors, as listed in the DSM-IV, pp. 93-94, include:

- Often loses temper
- Argues with adults
- Defiance and refusal to comply or cooperate with adult's requests or rules
- Deliberately annoys people
- Shuns personal responsibility and blames others for their mistakes and misbehaviors
- Angry and resentful

Behaviors of teens with ODD are aggravating and difficult for parents to control. One of the most difficult problems to cope with is their tendency to blame everyone and everything else for their mistakes. Even when there is irrefutable evidence of their having done something wrong, they will deny it or insist that it is not their fault. ODD has a pernicious and devastating effect on interpersonal relationships. Life with these individuals is like walking on eggshells, and symptoms frequently worsen with time in a vicious spiral of academic and relationship failure, with simultaneous lowering of self-esteem.

While it is the developmental job of all adolescents to be oppositional some of the time, the child with ODD is persistent and excessive, with these behaviors occurring much of the time, every day, and in many situations, putting considerable stress on the family. Sometimes the same medical treatment for AD/HD helps to relieve ODD symptoms as well. While treating AD/HD may reduce the ODD symptoms, they will usually reappear if medication is omitted or forgotten.

19

If these behaviors are seen in your teen, communicate this information to your child's physician. As with other high-risk behaviors, driving should be delayed until they have been successfully treated and parents are reasonably confident that the teen can handle driving safely.

"The essential feature of **Conduct Disorder** is repetitive and persistent patterns of behavior in which the basic rights of others or major age-appropriate societal norms or rules are violated. These behaviors fall into four main groupings: aggressive conduct that causes or threatens physical harm to other people or animals. . . nonaggressive conduct that causes property loss or damage. . . deceitfulness or theft. . . and serious violation of rules." (DSM-IV, pages 85-91).

1. Aggressive behaviors
    - Threatening or intimidating behavior (bullying), extortion
    - Initiation of physical fights
    - Use of a weapon
    - Cruelty to other people
    - Cruelty to animals
    - Stealing while confronting a victim (mugging, armed robbery)
    - Rape or forced sex with others

2. Deliberate destruction of property
    - Destroying property, including vandalism
    - Arson (fire setting)

3. Deceitful behaviors
    - Lying or stealing (shoplifting, forgery)
    - Breaking and entering

4. Serious violations of rules
    - Running away
    - Staying out at night, school truancy (before age 13)

For those parents whose children have Conduct Disorder as well as AD/HD, these behaviors are serious and deeply troubling. Parents may have tried all the suggestions of professionals to manage these behaviors and still see little improvement. We know through research that when both AD/HD and Conduct Disorder are present, an individual is more likely to abuse drugs; be suspended, expelled, or drop out of school; and become involved in the juvenile justice system.

Conduct Disorder has often been thought of as intentional behavior. More recently, however, researchers are showing that conduct disorder has an underlying biochemical cause. Some studies have linked these behaviors to subtle brain injury. In the past, many parents who did not know of effective treatments for conduct disorder have tired of the constant humiliation and criticism they receive because of their child's behavior. Many gave up trying to discipline the child, not knowing that treatment was available.

As the symptoms develop further, the very nature of the condition makes it hard for the adolescent to cooperate with suggested treatment. However, even at this stage, effective management is possible with a combination of medical and social interventions, provided the adolescent can be encouraged to see that there is something that can be done to help. Parents of children with both AD/HD and Conduct Disorder should very thoughtfully consider the complicating impact that driving will have in the child's life. Unless parents are able to gain consistent compliance with rules before the teen begins to drive, they may be setting their family up for long-term emotional and financial frustration, unhappiness, and involvement with the legal system. Treatment of this coexisting condition is critical for the personal safety of the teen and others.

Characteristics Associated with Mood or Affective Disorders

The overlap between AD/HD and depression occurs at a beyond-chance level, with some studies suggesting nearly 30% of children with AD/HD will also have depression. In clinical studies of depressed children, as many as 60% of the depressed children have symptoms of AD/HD. Depression can vary in severity from a moderate mood change known as dysthymia, to a major depressive or bipolar disorder. According to the DSM-IV, mood disorders can be classified into two major types: unipolar depressive disorder (clinical depression) and bipolar disorder (manic depressive disorder). If four or more of the symptoms of unipolar or bipolar depressive disorder are present for two weeks or longer, a physician or mental health professional should assess the individual.

The signs of **unipolar** or **clinical depression** often go unrecognized. They include:

- Inability to take pleasure in school, social activities, and hobbies
- Chronic feelings of hopelessness and worthlessness
- Loss of energy, constant tiredness, excessive sleeping
- Lack of appetite, excessive overeating, significant weight gain or loss
- Passive suicide attempts (risk-taking behaviors that could end in death not directly by one's own hand)

- "Pulling away" from friends (social withdrawal)
- Psychomotor agitation or retardation
- Frequent thoughts of death or suicide or suicide attempts
- Physical symptoms such as headaches and stomachaches

Parents and others in the teen's life may misinterpret depression as the youth being disinterested or insolent. Parents must be persistent in engaging with and monitoring the teen's behavior even when the teen doesn't show signs of cooperation or acknowledgment. Parents and health professionals must work together and be aware that it is not unusual for youth diagnosed with AD/HD to have the coexisting problems of depression.

Bipolar or **manic-depressive disorder** is a more severe and less common form of depression in youth. Bipolar disorder is characterized by symptoms that include an alternating pattern of emotional highs (manic episode) and emotional lows (depressive episode). Symptoms include:

- Psychotic behavior stemming from thoughts that seem to be out of touch with reality
- Increased risk for suicidal behaviors
- Irritability
- Hyperactivity
- Uncontrollable spending
- Rapid talking and body movements
- Abuse of chemical substances
- Compulsive and promiscuous sexual behaviors
- Manic phase is followed by severe clinical depression

Some years ago, it was not understood that children and adolescents could be depressed. As a result, depression was often overlooked and went untreated. It is now realized that bipolar disorder is not solely an adult problem, and that it can coexist with AD/HD. It should be considered as a possibility in children and adolescents with apparently severe AD/HD, especially when there are multiple complications, and/or persistent irritability. It should also be considered as a possibility in those who do not respond to conventional behavior management techniques. Young children may not exhibit the mood swings from mania to depression which are characteristic of adults, and thus may be difficult to diagnose accurately. The younger child with bipolar disorder tends to have extreme rages and irritability. The child may talk in a very rapid way, be persistently irritable, and have rage attacks. Often they have difficulty getting to sleep until late and they may have a number of other sleep problems.

Children who have attempted suicide need to be assessed not only for their depression, but also for the possibility of coexisting AD/HD. One study showed that adolescents who actually committed suicide had much higher rates of manic-depression and also of AD/HD than those who attempted suicide. The impulsiveness associated with AD/HD is extremely concerning when associated with severe depression.

Judy was a beautiful teen who was full of energy. Her parents were successful, well-respected community members. She was bright, bouncy, and popular with the kids because she was so "whimsical." She was a cheerleader all four years of her high school career. She was known, however, to be emotionally volatile and sometimes had severe mood swings. Sometimes when things didn't go right, she would retreat to her room for prolonged periods of isolation. Her school work varied from extremely good to extremely poor. One summer night, after having a "down spell" as well as breaking up with her boyfriend, Judy drove herself home from a baseball game.

Police estimated that Judy took a well-known curve in the highway at a speed of nearly 90 miles per hour. Her car was air borne for some time before crashing and rolling over and over down a hill. Judy was killed. Community members grieved her loss and felt certain that she used her parent's car as her means to commit suicide.

Characteristics Associated with Anxiety Disorders

Many individuals with AD/HD, particularly those with predominantly inattentive AD/HD, may have some symptoms of anxiety, although they may not fully meet the criteria for Anxiety Disorder. They may become anxious with change, especially over new situations or places; have problems with social or interpersonal failure or fears; experience panic attacks; and suffer from a wide range of generalized anxiety problems, any of which can be debilitating.

Generalized Anxiety Disorder is defined by three or more of the following characteristics:

- Edginess
- Muscle tension
- Mind going blank
- Irritability
- Fatigue
- Sleep disturbances

Panic Attacks usually start suddenly and involve a period of intense fear. Four or more of the following symptoms are characteristic of panic attacks:

- Pounding of heart
- Shortness of breath, feelings of being outside oneself (an observer)
- Chest discomfort
- Dizziness
- Fear of going crazy or losing control
- Trembling
- Nausea
- Tingling sensations throughout body or in extremities

If your teen is anxious about learning how to drive, you may need to seek professional help to develop a plan or process to gradually desensitize the fears that relate to the driving experience. The process takes time. Parents need to be patient. It is also important to understand that social anxiety or the fear of being rejected by peers can cause teens to take risks to show off and gain acceptance. In these situations, parents need to provide a great deal of structure and monitoring of their teen's activities.

Obsessive Compulsive Disorder (OCD) is associated with both obsessions (thoughts that keep reoccurring or repeating) and compulsions (repetitive behaviors that the person feels driven to do). Teens with OCD may need to have a very predictable schedule. They may also like and need routines, or indulge in compulsive hand washing or other ritual activities that are completed in the same way, time after time. They may not be able to sort and throw out trash, letting it pile up, or they may insist on a perfect environment.

Characteristics Associated with Alcohol/Substance Abuse

Professionals who work with alcohol/substance problems describe a range from *alcohol/substance use*, to *alcohol/substance abuse*, to *alcohol/substance dependence or addiction*. Alcohol/substance abuse is a progressive disease. The four stages of alcohol/substance involvement begin with experimental use of alcohol, cigarettes, and marijuana. Minor changes in the child's behavior are seen in the second stage. The next stage involves serious behavior problems such as rebelliousness, impulsive behavior, problems with the law, increased family conflict, and/or depression. The final stage is alcohol/substance dependence, where the teen feels that they need the alcohol/substance to feel normal. Parents should watch for physical signs such as increased skin problems, weight loss, unexplained injuries, fatigue, and sore throat. When a teen becomes alcohol/substance dependent, there is a risk of overdosing because of the increased amount and potency of the alcohol/substances being used.

It is now thought that teens with AD/HD and other coexisting conditions such as disruptive behavior disorders, anxiety, or depression often use alcohol or substances in an attempt to self-medicate to feel better. As in adults, teens may experience temporary euphoria or symptom relief, usually at the cost of greater problems.

Substance Abuse and Substance Dependence

Substance abuse is defined by the American Psychiatric Association in the DSM-IV, pp. 182-183, as a "maladaptive pattern of substance use, leading to clinically significant impairment or distress, as manifested by three or more of the following characteristics, occurring at any time in the same 12-month period. Characteristic problems include:

- Recurrent substance use resulting in a failure to fulfill major role obligations at work, school, or home (for example, repeated absences or poor work performance related to substance use; substance-related absences, suspensions, or expulsions from school; neglect of children or household)

- Recurrent substance use in situations in which it is physically hazardous (for example, driving an automobile or operating a machine when impaired by substance use)

- Recurrent substance-related legal problems (for example, arrests for substance-related disorderly conduct)

- Continued substance use despite having persistent or recurrent social or interpersonal problems caused or exacerbated by the effects of the substance (for example, arguments with spouse about consequences of intoxication, physical fights)

"Abuse" is often defined by experts as the "chronic use of any substance despite adverse social, psychological, or medical effects. This pattern of abuse may be intermittent or continuous and with or without physical dependence." For example, people who drink excessively once every few weeks and then drive are *abusing* alcohol even though they are not physically dependent on alcohol. Similarly, a teenager who smokes marijuana a few times a week after school and can't function at night to do homework is abusing the drug. Substance abuse, left untreated, will often lead to substance dependence, where the individual becomes physically dependent on the substance in order to function.

In the past, the condition of alcohol/substance abuse was regarded as a condition unto itself without the understanding that some people are more vulnerable to developing it than others. Effective management of AD/HD and/or coexisting conditions appears to help in the management of substance abuse.

About Inhalants

Because inhalants are readily available and relatively cheap, they are especially popular among children and young adolescents. These drugs are dangerous and potentially lethal. Parents should be aware that the average age when children try inhalants is around 13, and that children who use inhalants often "graduate" to other substances and stronger drugs.

Inhalants are drugs that produce a quick, temporary high. Individuals experience light-headedness and euphoria when the fumes or gases are breathed and absorbed into the body through the lungs. Because the high is usually mild and short-lived, many abusers believe that inhalants are harmless. They are wrong! Inhalants can be very dangerous, both in their short-term and long-term effects.

The high is sometimes compared to the sensation of being drunk. The high from inhalants tends to last only a short time, from a few minutes to about three-quarters of an hour. Aftereffects are often similar to an alcohol hangover, and the headache, nausea, or drowsiness can last for a couple of hours. During the high itself and for a period of time afterward, physical coordination and mental judgment are impaired, the same as with the use of alcohol. Abusers often suffer falls and other accidents. They may engage in irresponsible or dangerous behavior and certainly cannot drive safely.

Heavy use of inhalants can cause serious long-term effects. Each time the child uses inhalants, it seems that tolerance for the inhalant increases. Larger doses are needed to produce the same results. Heavy doses in turn increase the likelihood of permanent brain damage, with major effects such as poor memory, extreme mood swings, tremors, and seizures. Heavy, continuous use also increases the risk of heart arrhythmia and respiratory depression.

Signs of inhalant abuse include:

- A sweet, chemical smell on the clothes or body
- Unusual breath odor
- Correction fluid on nose, fingers, or clothing, or markers in pockets
- Lack of concentration
- Irritability

- Inflammation of the nostrils, frequent nosebleeds
- Sores around the mouth
- Poor appetite and loss of weight
- Pale, bluish skin
- Watery, bloodshot eyes with dilated pupils
- Slow, slurred speech or clumsy, staggering gait, and drunken appearance
- Frequent headaches
- Deterioration of school grades

Implications for Parents

Parenting teens with AD/HD will give the best of parents many unexpected challenges. AD/HD has many different manifestations and we should not expect to find a single, simple solution to those challenges. Each person's treatment needs to be tailored to address their specific problems. Issues will change over the years as the secondary complications of educational and emotional difficulty overlay the original symptoms of AD/HD. Frequent power struggles over homework or chores, and physical or verbal hostility make parenting teens with AD/HD very stressful. Because they do not necessarily respond to traditional management techniques, these teens tend to be criticized and punished more than others do. This can lead to hardened attitudes for both the parents and the teen. One or both parents may also have AD/HD, and this can compound oppositional behavior and relationship problems. It was found by Walker that in 81% of the parent pairs of children with AD/HD, at least one of the parents had AD/HD.

Although parents look forward to placing greater trust in their children and allowing them to become more independent once they become teenagers, parents of teens with AD/HD realize that this is not always possible. Immaturity, impulsivity, and other AD/HD symptoms lead to many difficulties which compound family stress. Parents know or sense this, but are not sure what to do. Not surprisingly, there is a high incidence of parental separation and divorce in such circumstances. Living with a teenager with AD/HD, with or without coexisting disorders, is a daily challenge that places enormous pressure on parental skills and judgment. Teaching a teen with AD/HD to demonstrate safe driving behaviors can be accomplished, but it takes every bit of skill, judgment, and patience that parents can muster in order to do so.

Driving statistics for teens with and without AD/HD and coexisting disorders are shocking. Parents must employ every reasonable means to treat AD/HD and coexisting disorders before allowing their teens to drive. Failure to do so is a prescription for disaster.

Parent and Teen Activity:

1. Reread through the lists of characteristics of AD/HD and any coexisting disorder diagnosed in your teen. As you read through the lists of behaviors for diagnosis of these conditions, think about how these behaviors would impact driving behavior. Place a check mark beside those characteristics that will help your child to be an attentive and safe driver.

   NOTE: Unfortunately, there are no characteristics listed in any of the above disorders that are going to be an asset to your teen as they learn to drive. The behavioral characteristics negatively affected by AD/HD are the ones you need the most for safe driving!

2. Go back through the list of characteristics of AD/HD and any coexisting disorder diagnosed in your teen. Check the characteristics that will be beneficial to you, as a parent, in teaching your teen how to drive.

   NOTE: The very characteristics that define AD/HD, Learning Disabilities, Oppositional Defiant Disorder, Conduct Disorder, or Alcohol/Substance Abuse are also characteristics that predict more difficulty in learning new skills. These characteristics also lead to frustrating parent-child relationships. Parents must clearly understand that teens with AD/HD need more supervised practice and monitoring to learn and sustain safe driving behaviors than teens without these problems. Parents must also recognize that when a teen has coexisting disorders along with AD/HD, this process may be even more difficult.

   Ignoring the characteristic behaviors of these conditions, shunning effective treatment options, and placing your child in the drivers seat is a predictable prescription for disaster.

Reasonable Parent Expectations

Parents need to encourage their teenagers with AD/HD to do their best as they learn to drive. We must do all we can to help them adopt safe driving attitudes and behaviors. But parents need to accept the fact that it is not a catastrophe when sons or daughters fail to achieve perfection. Minor fender benders, dents, and door dings happen to most drivers. When they happen to our children, it doesn't mean they're headed for certain ruination or that they are purposefully trying to anger us. Even after working diligently to coach their adolescents and after following all the suggestions set forth in this book, parents should not expect their teens with AD/HD to be perfect drivers. It is realistic, however, to expect them to try their best.

It's unrealistic to expect your son or daughter to never get speeding tickets, for example, but it is realistic to hold the teen responsible for paying for the ticket and to complying with medication schedules that will help the teen attend to monitoring driving speed and better coordinate "motor skills." It's especially unrealistic to expect your teenager to always come to a complete stop for highway signs if you are constantly rolling through stop signs. It's even unrealistic to expect your teen to never have an accident, but it is realistic for parents to expect teens to do their best to comply with family and traffic rules when they are behind the wheel.

References:

Amen, D. (1996). *Windows into the ADD Mind.* Fairfield, CA: Mind Works Press.

American Psychiatric Association. (1994). *Diagnostic and Statistical Manual of Mental Disorders. Fourth Edition.* (DSM-IV) Washington, DC.

Barkley, R. (1998). *Attention Deficit Hyperactivity Disorder: A Handbook for Diagnosis and Treatment. Second Edition.* New York and London: Guilford Press.

Garfinkel, B. *et al.* (1994). Major Affective Disorders in Children and Adolescents. Winokur, G. (Ed.) *The Medical Basis of Psychiatry.* W. B. Saunders Co.

Goldstein, S. and Goldstein, M. (1998). *Managing Attention Deficit Hyperactivity Disorder in Children: A Guide for Practitioners. Second Edition.* New York: John Wiley and Sons, Inc.

Ingersoll, B. and Goldstein, S. (1995). *Lonely, Sad and Angry: A Parent's Guide to Depression in Children and Adolescents.* New York: Doubleday.

Kewley, G. D. (1999). *Attention Deficit Hyperactivity Disorder: Recognition, Reality and Resolution.* LAC Press, 2nd Floor, 44 Springfiled Road, Horsham, W. Sussex RH 12 2 PD, UK.

McClelland, J. M., Rubert, M. P., Reichler, R. J., and Sylvester, C. E. (1989). Attention deficit disorder in children at risk for anxiety and depression. *Journal of the American Academy of Child and Adolescent Psychiatry,* 29, 534-539.

PACER Center, Inc. (2000). *Unique Challenges, Hopeful Responses: A Handbook for Professionals Working with Youth with Disabilities in the Juvenile Justice System.*

Slaby, A. and Garfinkel, L. (1994). *No One Saw My Pain: Why Teens Kill Themselves.* New York and London: W.W. Norton and Company.

Swanson, J., et. al., (1998, Apr.) Cognitive Neuroscience of Attention Deficit Hyperactivity Disorder and Hyperkinetic Disorder. *Current Opinion – In Neurobiology, 8* (2), 263-271.

Walker, C. W. (1999). *Prevalence of Adult ADHD Symptoms in Parents of ADHD Children.* California School of Professional Psychology, Fresno, CA. Dissertation.

Zametkin, A. J., et al. (1990, Nov. 15). Cerebral Glucose Metabolism in Adults with Hyperactivity of Childhood Onset. *The New England Journal of Medicine,* 323 (20), 1361.

Miller, D. and Blum, K. (1996). *Overload: Attention Deficit Disorder and the Addictive Brain.* Kansas City, MO: Andrews and McMeel.

Resources on Teens with AD/HD:

Barkley, R. (1991). Video: *ADHD - What Can We Do?* New York: Guilford Press.

Barkley, R. (1991). Video: *ADHD - What Do We Know?* New York: Guilford Press.

Barkley, R. (1995). *Taking Charge of AD/HD: The Complete Authoritative Guide for Parents,* New York: Guilford Press.

Barkley, R. (1997). *AD/HD and the Nature of Self-Control.* New York: Guilford Press.

Barkley, R. (2000). *A New Look at AD/HD: Inhibition, Time and Self Control.* New York: Guilford Press.

Brown, T. E. (2000). *Attention Deficit Disorders and Comorbidities in Children, Adolescents and Adults.* Washington, DC: American Psychiatric Press.

CHADD (1996). *ADD and Adolescence: Strategies for Success from CHADD.* 8181 Professional Place, Landover, MD 20785.

Dornbush, M. P. and Pruitt, S. K. (1995). *Teaching the Tiger.* Duarte, CA: Hope Press.

DuPaul, G. and Stoner, G. (1999). *AD/HD in the Schools: Assessment and Intervention Strategies,* Guilford School Practitioners Series. New York: Guilford Press.

Gordon, M. (1992). *I Would If I Could: A Teenagers Guide to AD/HD Hyperactivity.* DeWitt, NY: GSI Publications.

Nadeau, K., Littman, E. B., and Quinn, P. (2000). *Understanding Girls with AD/HD.* Silver Spring, MD: Advantage Books.

Parker, H. (1998). *Putting Yourself in Their Shoes: Understanding Where Your AD/HD Teen Is Coming From.* Plantation, FL: Specialty Press.

Parker, H. (2000). *Problem Solver Guide for Students with AD/HD.* Plantation, FL: Specialty Press.

Reif, S. (1993). *How to Reach and Teach AD/HD Children: Practical Techniques, Strategies, and Interventions for Helping Children With Attention Problems and Hyperactivity.* Nyack, New York: The Center for Applied Research in Education.

Robin, A. (1998). *AD/HD in Adolescents: Diagnosis and Treatment.* New York: Guilford Press.

Zeigler, C. A. Dendy. (2000). *Teaching Teens with ADD and AD/HD: A Quick Reference Guide for Teachers and Parents.* Bethesda, MD: Woodbine House.

Zeigler, C. A. Dendy. (1995). *Teenagers with ADD.* Bethesda, MD: Woodbine House.

National Organizations:

Children & Adults with Attention Deficit Hyperactivity Disorder (CHADD)
8181 Professional Drive, Suite 202, Lanham, MD 20706, (800) 233-4050
Website: www.chadd.org

Attention Deficit Disorders Association (ADDA)
P.O. Box 1303, Northbrook, IL 60065, (216) 350-9595
Website: www.adda.org

Learning Disabilities Association of America (LDAA)
4156 Library Road, Pittsburgh, PA 15234, (412) 341-1515
Website: www.ldanatl.org

National Information Center for Children and Youth with Disabilities
P.O. Box 1492, Washington, DC 20013-1492, (800) 695-0285
Website: www.nichcy.org

Parent Advocacy Center for Educational Rights (PACER)
8161 Normandale Blvd., Minneapolis, MN 55437, (952) 838-9000
Website: www.pacer.org

Chapter 3

General Tips for Parenting Teens with Difficult Behaviors

Talk to Your Children About Driving Safely

Children Now and the Kaiser Family Foundation, both part of a national campaign to support parents, have produced a manual written by Lynn Dumas entitled, "How to Talk with Your Kids About......". The manual presents ten tips for talking to children about tough, life-threatening issues such as alcohol, drugs, violence, and HIV/AIDS. With some adaptation, these ten tips, set forth below, can be useful for parents to talk to their children about another life-threatening issue–teen driving. The single most important protective factor is your relationship with your child and expressing clear expectations with respect to their driving.

1. Start early.
When children want information, advice, and guidance, they turn to their parents first. Once they reach the teenage years, however, they tend to depend more on friends, the media, and others for their information. Children between the ages of 6 and 12 are interested in what you do. Talk to them about driving and teach them about driving safety before they express an interest in driving and are old enough to get a learner's permit.

2. Initiate conversations with your child.
Don't expect your children to ask questions about driving when they are very young, but be observant as to what they are experiencing in their environment, and speak to them about it. With driving, these conversations can start very early. As an example, when you drive, speak to them about the importance of driving safely. Talk to them about why you come to a complete stop at stop signs, why you insist they use their seat belts, why young children ride in the back seat, and why it's important for

drivers to be considerate of pedestrians. Point out the mistakes you observe in other drivers, and talk about why it's important to keep an eye on other drivers.

3. Talk about topics that are uncomfortable for you.
Share newspaper accounts of motor vehicle collisions. Don't shield your child from knowing that young children and teens are often killed in automobile crashes. Perhaps someone you know will experience the loss of a beloved pet to a careless driver. Discuss how those deaths or serious injuries will impact family members. Stress the importance of driving safely so that others are not hurt.

4. Create an open environment.
Our children want parents to discuss adult subjects with them. It's up to us, as parents, to create the kind of atmosphere in which our children can ask any question — on any subject — freely and without fear of being laughed at, put down, or given wrong information.

5. Communicate your values.
As a parent, you have the opportunity to be the first person to talk with your children about important issues such as driving. Talk to them early, before anyone else can confuse them with contradictory information that lacks the sense of values and moral principles you want to instill. Do you want them to learn from your values about driving, or develop values more influenced by their peers? Let your children know that character counts when driving a vehicle. Talk about courtesy, patience, and respect for others. Even when you think that teens and children with AD/HD are not listening, they probably are. Keep talking!

6. Listen to your child.
It's important to find time to give our kids our undivided attention. Listening carefully to our children builds their self-esteem by letting them know that they're important to us. Listening to them can lead to valuable discussions about a wide variety of issues. Listen, to understand their concerns or misperceptions about driving issues.

7. Try to be honest.
Whatever their age, your children deserve honest answers and explanations. When we don't provide straightforward answers to their questions, we undermine our children's ability to trust us. If you don't know the answer to a question, say so, and help your child to find the answer.

8. Be patient.
When parenting children with AD/HD and other difficult behaviors,

patience is a very important virtue to develop! As adults, we may be tempted to rush to supply answers before our children have the opportunity to fully explain what they need. Try to resist this impulse. Sometimes teens with difficult behaviors have a hard time putting their thoughts into proper sequence, or they get frustrated by not being able to find the best words to use. By listening patiently, we allow our children to think at their own pace and we let them know that they are worthy of our time.

9. Use everyday opportunities to talk.

Teens tend to resist formal discussions about important issues, often categorizing them as just another lecture from mom and dad. You can use moments that arise in everyday life as "talk opportunities," when your children will be far less likely to tune you out. For instance, a television commercial about cars can provide an opportunity to talk about the kind of car that has a good safety rating.

10. Talk about it again.

And, again! Most young people (and especially individuals with AD/HD) typically won't learn all they need to know about a particular topic from a single discussion. If individuals are extremely interested in the topic, their attention will be longer. It's important to let a little time pass, then ask the child to tell you what he remembers about your previous conversation. Then bring up the topic again. You may need to cover some important points about driving over and over again. Patience and persistence will serve you and your child well.

Set Clear Rules

Rules and limits for the young driver are necessary to create order within the family. The lack of rules or limits for a young driver will create chaos and confusion for everyone. Rules provide the basis for understanding what is expected of the teen. If harmony is to be maintained within the family, there must be a proper set of family rules, understandings, and expectations that are based on your family values. If your teen is usually compliant and responsible, you will probably need only a few rules. However, if you are dealing with a difficult or defiant teen, you are already familiar with the need for more clearly defined structure.

When setting rules that extend to a teen's driving behaviors, parents will want to identify some basic **core rules** and then support the core rules by establishing several small **preventative rules.**

35

Example 1:

If you want your teen to stay away from alcohol or drug use, the core rule is:

"You are not allowed to use alcohol or drugs."

Preventative rules that you will need to add to support the core rule address:

- **WHO** your teen may associate with;
- **WHAT** types of activities are allowed;
- **WHERE** your teen is allowed to go;
- **WHEN** your teen may go; and
- **WHEN** your teen will return.

When the teen is old enough to drive, one of the consequences for abusing alcohol or drugs is the loss of the driving privilege. The consequences should be clearly stated:

"If you drink alcohol or use drugs, you will not be allowed to drive."

It's naive for parents to think that their teens can be safe drivers if they hang around in the wrong places or associate with high-risk, alcohol or drug-using friends.

Example 2:

If you want your teen to be successful at school, the core rule is:

"You will complete your high school education."

Preventative rules that you will need to support this core rule are:

- You will attend school every day;
- Homework will be done daily;
- Weekly progress reports will be positive;
- Acceptable school grades will be maintained; and
- School behavior must be positive.

Rather than waiting for the mid-semester or end-of-semester reports, parents must set rules and create the structure that will help their teens along the way and maximize their chances for success.

Creating preventative rules to support your core rules provides your teen with a clear understanding of expectations. Preventative rules allow parents to be involved with their teen so that they can be aware of problems early and resolve them, before they become overwhelming for both the teens and the parents.

Regarding driving, one of the consequences for poor school performance can be, "If you are failing any of your classes, you will not be allowed to apply for a driver's license."

You may have heard some folks say, "Take care of little troubles before they become big ones." This is good advice for parents working with difficult teen behaviors. Conflict is inevitable with difficult or defiant teens. Consistently addressing and resolving conflicts over small issues such as homework, dress, grooming, negligent driving, and curfew is your best preventative course of action in avoiding the larger issues of dropping out of school, alcohol or drug abuse, delinquent behavior, or teen parenthood.

Teen Compliance with the Rules

Once you have established your rules, teen compliance is not likely unless:

- The teen clearly understands the rules;
- The parent is monitoring compliance with the rules;
- The parent is consistently enforcing the rules;
- The parent is administering the predetermined consequences; and
- The consequences are meaningful deterrents to the teen.

Understanding the Rules

If your rules are not clearly understood, it leaves a lot of room for misunderstandings, conflicts, and even manipulations. Many parents assume that the teen understands the rules in the same way they are intended. For example, if you tell your teen, "You may take the family car, but you must be home early," the teen's interpretation of "early" may be dramatically different from yours. Your rules need to be very specific. It would be better to say, "You may take the family car, but you must be home by 8:30." To avoid misunderstanding, it's a good policy to have your teen write down the rule or restate the rule to demonstrate clear understanding of your rule or expectations.

Parental Monitoring

Parents provide a safety net for their children by monitoring their behavior, just as state troopers provide a safety net for drivers by monitoring their behavior on the highway. How much monitoring a parent should do depends on how much monitoring is needed. Some teens require very little monitoring while difficult teens with high-risk behaviors require a great deal of parental monitoring. Let your teen know that you will be monitoring for both appropriate and inappropriate behavior. This will do a couple of things. First, they should not be surprised that you are monitoring. Second, being aware of the monitoring practice provides added incentive for the teen to follow the rules.

Consistent, careful monitoring of a teen's behavior will help parents to detect early clues to problems that their teens may be struggling with, such as alcohol or substance abuse, school failure, or sexual pressures from peers. When a parent is alert to the signs of problems, they can seek help at the early stages of teen troubles. The following points are important basics in a program of teen monitoring:

- Always get to know your child's friends. Invite them over to the house.

- Don't allow your child to go out with a group of peers you don't know or don't trust.

- Introduce yourself to the parents of your child's friends. They may also have concerns about their teen and you can help support each other when concerned about the behaviors of your teens.

- You can't be home all the time, so get to know your neighbors and ask them to alert you when there may be a problem going on at your home.

- Be unpredictable in your own schedule. Come home early sometimes.

- Don't give permission for your teen to drive to or to stay over at another person's house if you suspect alcohol or substance abuse in either individual.

- Contact your child's teachers to be sure that schoolwork is satisfactory and that they have not observed troublesome behaviors.

- Make it a point to always be at home at your teen's curfew time. Stay awake and keep the lights on in the house until your child comes home.

- Always hug your children when they come home. Be alert to any residual smells of marijuana, alcohol, or smoke. Be alert to smells of cologne and chewing gum that are often used to try to cover up other odors.

- If your children go directly to their rooms when they come home from being out with friends, follow them and start a conversation. Observe their overall behavior, speech, communication patterns, balance, and coordination.

- Don't allow yourself to ever be kept out of your teen's room. Parents can respect a teen's privacy without giving up the right to enter the teen's room when you are concerned about safety.

- Pay attention to your child's language. Substance abuse brings with it a specific culture and vocabulary. It is important that parents know the language that teens use when talking about substance use. For example, words used to describe alcohol include booze, brain grenade, hooch, and paint. Marijuana references include pot, grass, dank, smoke, buds, trees, Mary Jane, weed, Colombian, reefer, and joint. Cocaine nicknames include coke, snow, nose, flake, blow, line, C, and powder. Rock cocaine is referred to as crack, rock, base, and Roxanne. Amphetamines are often called crank, bennies, splash, peaches, crystal, meth, speed, water, and black beauties. Heroin is often called Big H, smack, brown sugar, tar, mud, thing, or horse. LSD may be referred to as acid, barrels, blue sugar, blotter, tabs, squares, or windowpanes. New words and descriptors come up from time to time, so if your teens use words you don't understand, ask them about the meaning of those words. Sign up and take your teen to a drug or alcohol abuse prevention program in your community.

Proactive monitoring of teen driving behaviors can happen in a number of ways.

- Involve your neighbors and friends in observing your teen's driving behaviors and reporting back to you both the positive and negative incidents that they observe.

- The use of the vehicle can be monitored through odometer checks.

- If you have ever wondered if your teen was speeding in your car, or if your teen took the car without your permission there are now ways to check. Advanced technology allows you to add equipment to your car that can give you a readout about the speeds your vehicle has been traveling and the time of day the vehicle was traveling at those speeds. Electronic devices can be integrated with the car's mechanical systems. Check out website www.easesim.com/autowatch_parents.htm or contact AutoWatch, EASE Simulation, Inc., State Route 492, Box 3011, New Milford, PA 18834.

- Make unannounced checks of the contents of the vehicle.

- Teen driver monitoring services provide a unique method for parents to monitor behavior of the newly licensed teen driver. The car the teen drives is registered with the monitoring service. Parents receive a sticker to apply to the registered car. The sticker clearly displays a toll-free number that can be called to alert parents to observed driving behaviors. Parents are informed of reports by email, fax, or regular mail. This gives the parent and teen an opportunity to discuss the circumstances of the report and decide upon appropriate action. You may find national teen monitoring services on the web. Two that have been in business for several years are: 4 My Teen, PO Box 172225, Arlington, TX 76003-225. Their website is www.4myteen.org or phone 1-800-469-8836. If you live in Canada, contact the I Promise Program, 20 Suter Crescent, Dundas, Ontario L9H6R5.
Website: www.papyrusgraphix.com/ipp/ipp-contract.pdf

- You can closely monitor your teen's driving curfew times.

- You can check with the parents of your teen's friends to be sure of the date and time of the teen's activities.

- You can drive by locations of special activities to be sure that your teens are where they are supposed to be.

Consistent Enforcement of the Rules

The hardest, yet most important thing parents can do is to be consistent in their monitoring of rules and in their administration of logical consequences for rule infractions. If rules are not enforced, it's the same as not having any rules. In order for teens to feel safe and protected, they need to know that they can count on their parents to be consistent and dependable. If a violation of a rule occurs, parents need to consistently enforce the previously established consequence. A teen with AD/HD or other difficult behaviors will test the boundaries to see what their limits will truly be. That is why parental monitoring and consistency are so important.

If, at the beginning of a teen's driving career, parents let small things slide until they become big things, then chaos, confusion, and resentment will be the end result. While most parents do let some small things go from time to time, it's a very ineffective approach. Being hard-nosed and especially consistent with driving rules and consequences while the teen is learning to drive will save a lot of battling over the rules at a later time. Consistency is the key. Follow through on what you said you would do.

Write out your rules and their consequences. Sporadic enforcement does not work. Remember, only those parents who consistently monitor and enforce their rules will have their rules consistently followed.

Administer Meaningful Consequences Immediately

Research has shown that immediate consequences for youth with AD/HD are the most effective. They have a tendency to not think about the rule they have violated if the consequences are delayed. Immediate consequences are those disciplinary actions taken on the spot, when rules are broken, before the teen can resume any normal activities. Immediate consequences might include such things as time-out, room restriction, a work project, or a special assignment. If you don't have an immediate consequence, teens often focus on the person who administers delayed consequences rather than the rule that was violated. This often happens if teens with AD/HD are required to go to court for driving violations. By the time the court date arrives, they have forgotten what got them into trouble, and instead turn their focus toward finding unfairness from the parent or the justice system for taking away privileges.

Follow-up consequences are those applied over a specific period of time such as the loss of driving privileges, a major work project, being grounded, a loss of telephone privileges, additional household chores, or loss of a planned upcoming activity. Consequences for breaking rules must be strong enough to be effective deterrents for such behavior in the future.

Parents have the sole responsibility for determining and administering the consequences for inappropriate behavior. Consequences will vary depending on the severity of the violation as well as on the teen's response to the consequence. Some teens may respond to the loss of the privilege of going out on Saturday night, while others may not be bothered by that consequence at all. Parents must use consequences that have significant meaning and/or deterrent value for their teen. The challenge for parents is to find the right balance in order to get the teen to want to comply with the rules.

Illustration by Vicente Utrera

41

Parent with Dignity

Mac and Barbara Bledsoe, authors of the "Parenting With Dignity" parent training video series, eloquently teach parents the difference between parental authority established through positive discipline and through ineffective punishments. Discipline is used to teach children what they did wrong and how they should correct their actions to behave more appropriately in the future.

Punishment almost always removes the focus of both the parent (punisher) and the teen (punishee) from the behavior in question. Anger takes over and interrupts responsible thought. The teen focuses their anger on the punisher rather than coming to terms with their inappropriate behaviors. Parents sometimes focus on the punishment and the teen's reaction to punishment rather than focusing their child's attention to face reasonable and known consequences for their actions.

Parental monitoring, consistent enforcement of the rules, and consistent administration of logical consequences are all aspects of positive parental discipline. Requiring your teen to experience consequences for unsafe driving behaviors is important. It is not reasonable to let your teen experience incarceration, loss of dignity, a major injury or death when you can step in early to teach safe behaviors to prevent such outcomes.

Act, don't Yak!

Dr. Sam Goldstein, a behavioral psychologist, points out that parents often talk too much instead of taking action. He advises, "Act, don't yak!" He encourages parents of children with AD/HD not to sermonize, lecture, demean, or try to induce guilt — just administer the consequences immediately and consistently. Negotiation fuels the fire for a manipulative adolescent. The more they talk and get you to talk, the greater the likelihood someone will start negotiating and compromising. Some negotiation may be okay for small issues, but not on issues that have to do with core values or safety!

In his book, *Put Yourself in Their Shoes*, Harvey Parker, Ph.D., offers advice for preventing teens from manipulating their parents. He says parents should determine consequences for breaking their rules and stick to them. Don't be talked out of your behavioral expectations and don't accept excuses from your child. Be persistent and follow through. Apologies from the teen are important, but they shouldn't excuse behavior or replace a consequence. Accept the apology, but follow through with appropriate consequences.

Don't waiver on important issues.

If the consequences you have given for breaking rules are not effective, they will be ignored by your teen. Some teens will not respond regardless of the consequences imposed. Other teens may defiantly refuse to comply with the consequences. If either of these situations should happen to you, withdraw all teen driving privileges immediately. Take control of the keys of all vehicles. Parents may need to get professional help from outside sources in working with a difficult teen's behavior. Getting teens to comply with rules often requires changes in both the parents' and the teen's established behavior patterns. Don't ignore the problem, thinking that it will go away. Little problems do grow up to be big problems. Defiance and driving are a deadly duo.

References:

Children Now, 1212 Broadway, Fifth Floor, Oakland, CA 94612

Drew Bledsoe Foundation. (1997). *Parenting with Dignity.*
Website: www.drewbledsoe.com

Dumas, L. S. *How to Talk with Your Kids About Tough Issues.*
Children Now and Kaiser Family Foundation.
(For a free booklet, call 1-800-CHILD44.)
Website: www.talkingwithkids.org

Kaiser Family Foundation, 2400 Sand Hill Road, Menlo Park, CA 94025.

Parker, H. (1999). *Put Yourself in Their Shoes: Understanding Teenagers with Attention Deficit Hyperactivity Disorder.* Plantation, FL: Specialty Press, Inc.

Goldstein, S., Goldstein, M. and Wiley, W. (1987). *Hyperactivity: Why Won't My Child Pay Attention?*

Chapter 4

20 Steps for Parents to Promote Safe Driving Behaviors in Teens with AD/HD

This chapter first lists the 20 steps, then considers each step in more detail. Completing these steps will not totally insure the teen's safety, but will enhance the likelihood that your teen will have a safe driving experience. The first ten steps should be completed before the teen is allowed to sit in the driver's seat. Even though the process looks logical and easy to accomplish, getting through the 20 steps is not a quick or easy process. The 20 steps impose expectations on both parents and teens. Some teens will require more time than others to meet expectations. Parents of teens with severe AD/HD or coexisting conditions may find this process takes a few months or even a few years to accomplish. Briefly, the steps are:

1. Model safe driving behaviors.

2. Address AD/HD and any coexisting conditions or behavior problems your teen may have that will impact your teen's ability to drive safely.

3. Determine the maturity/driving readiness of your teen.

4. Familiarize yourself and your teen with your state's driving laws.

5. Select driver education materials and plan the content of your teen's driving lessons.

6. Consider medication issues and driving safety.

7. Establish an incentive system for teens to earn time to practice driving.

8. Discuss safe driving expectations with your teen and create a teen driving contract which outlines important agreements to be honored during the time the teen is driving with a learner's permit.

9. Select the vehicle that you will allow your teen to use while learning to drive.

10. Make all necessary insurance arrangements.

11. Apply for the learner's permit only when you and your teen are ready to assume the responsibilities involved.

12. Permit your teenager to sign up for a driver education class at school, but do not abdicate parental responsibility to the school for teaching your teen how to drive safely.

13. Carry out the driving lesson plans you have developed.

14. Evaluate the driving skills of your teen and provide feedback during and after each lesson. Monitor all agreements in the Learner's Permit Contract.

15. After basic driving skills have been mastered, expose the teen driver to various driving conditions and prepare for potential driving emergencies.

16. When all instruction and evaluation have been completed satisfactorily, prepare your teen for the driver's license examination.

17. Negotiate a new contract for after the teen is licensed.

18. Contact your insurance agent again to be sure the teen is covered when driving with a graduated or unrestricted license.

19. When responsible, safe driving behaviors have been demonstrated and good habits have been established, allow your teen to apply for the driver's license .

20. After the driver's license has been issued, continue to monitor the teen's driving behaviors, administer consequences as needed, and insist that all contract agreements be honored.

Step #1
Model safe driving behaviors.

"Children are natural mimics–they act like their parents in spite of every attempt to teach them good habits." -Anonymous

Parents need to remember that in driving, as with all other life activities, your children are watching you and learning from your actions. When you drive, set a good example. Your actions and driving behaviors speak louder than words! Talk the talk and walk the walk! Consider your teen's confusion when you say, "Obey the speed limits," and then you use a radar detector to avoid speeding tickets. What is the message your teen receives when you say, "Pay close attention to your driving," yet you use a cellular phone when you drive?

Would you be comfortable if your teenager drove as you do? Take a minute to consider your own driving habits. You should be able to respond "yes" to all of the following statements.

Yes	No	Parent Driving Behavior Checklist
		1. I remain calm in frustrating driving situations.
		2. I treat other drivers with the same respect I would like to get from them.
		3. I observe and obey all speed limits.
		4. I always come to a full stop for stop signs.
		5. I never drive when using alcohol or other drugs which could impair my ability to drive.
		6. I always wear a seat belt.
		7. I never drive when I am sleepy.
		8. I know the significance of all traffic signs and follow their warnings.
		9. I have a safe driving record.

AD/HD is Most Often an Inherited Condition

AD/HD is now understood to most often be a genetic, lifelong condition. For a majority of individuals, AD/HD symtoms do not go away in adolescence. Untreated AD/HD can impact driving behaviors well into adulthood. If you are the biological parent of a teen with AD/HD and are unable to answer "yes" to all of the statements listed above, there is a chance that you may have experienced some driving safety issues of your own related to AD/HD. A list of resources about AD/HD in adults is located at the end of this section.

Adults with AD/HD may find it difficult to teach their children how to drive. They may lack the patience they need to give helpful instruction. Also, the parent with AD/HD may not be a licensed driver. Untreated adults with AD/HD may have had to surrender their license for numerous traffic violations. Sometimes adults with AD/HD simply cannot afford the repair bills and insurance rates associated with their poor driving records.

Adults Who Teach Must Have a Valid Driver's License

Don't ignore the fact that adults who are instructing teens to drive on a learner's permit must have a **valid driver's license.** If you do not have a driver's license, you will need to enlist the help of a qualified licensed adult to work with your teen. However, this does not mean that you should not be involved in the process. Teens can learn a great deal from parents who have experienced difficulty in their own lives. Parents without a valid driver's license can still be involved with other parts of the safe driver training process. It's important to be honest with your teen and to not blame others for your own driving failures. Encourage your teen to not make the same mistakes that you made!

Resources About AD/HD in Adults

Barkley, R. (1994). Video: *ADHD in Adults.* New York: Guilford Press.

Barkley, R. (1997). *AD/HD and the Nature of Self-Control.* New York: Guilford Press.

Fowler, R. and Fowler, J. (1995). *Honey, Are You Listening?* Nashville, TN: Thomas Wilson.

Hallowell, E. and Ratey, J. (1994). *Driven to Distraction.* New York: Pantheon Books.

Kelly, K., Ramundo, P., and Ledingham S., (1997). *The ADDed Dimension: Everyday Advice for Adults with ADD.* New York: Scribner.

Murphy, K. and LeVert, S. (1995). *Out of the Fog: Treatments Options and Coping Strategies for Adult Attention Deficit Disorder.* New York: Hyperion.

Nadeau, K. G. (1997). *ADD in the Workplace: Choices, Changes, and Challenges.* Silver Spring, MD: Advantage Books.

Novatni, M. (2000). *What Does Everybody Else Know That I Don't?* Plantation, FL: Specialty Press.

Roberts, M.S. and Jansen, G. J., (1997). *Living with ADD: A Workbook for Adults with Attention Deficit Disorder.* Oakland, CA: New Harbinger.

Solden, S. (1995). *Women with Attention Deficit Disorder.* Grass Valley, CA: Underwood Books.

Wender, P. (2000). *AD/HD: Attention Deficit Hyperactivity Disorder in Children and Adults.* New York: Oxford University Press.

Wiess, M., Trokenberg-Hectman, L., and Weiss, G. *AD/HD in Adulthood: A Guide to Current Theory, Diagnosis, and Treatment.*

Step #2
Address AD/HD and any coexisting conditions or behavior problems your teen may have that will impact your teen's ability to drive safely.

"When you think of attention deficit disorder, visualize the iceberg with only one-eighth of its mass visible above the water line. As is true of icebergs, often the most challenging aspects of AD/HD are hidden beneath the surface." -Chris A. Zeigler Dendy, M.S.

Addressing AD/HD and Coexisting Disorders

Learning to drive safely is a serious and substantial task for any adolescent. When the difficulty of the task is magnified through neurological or behavioral problems, then the parents and the teen must make efforts to understand these complications and work together to minimize the additional risks involved. Problems with any coexisting disorders such as anger control, alcohol or substance abuse, or other diagnosed conditions should be addressed with appropriate treatments before you allow your teen to drive.

Treatment interventions that have proven to be beneficial for AD/HD and other high-risk behaviors include parent training, individual and family counseling, behavior management techniques, educational interventions, and medication. The attentive administration of a prescribed medication program has been shown to be one of the most effective components of treatment for AD/HD symptoms.

Addressing Anger Issues

The American Automobile Association (AAA) Foundation for Traffic Safety warns American drivers that "road rage", driving influenced by aggression and/or anger, is a growing public concern. More and more drivers have started acting out their anger when they get behind the wheel of a motor vehicle. The AAA Foundation has identified four components of road rage.

1) Anger or irritation with other drivers' behaviors or highway traffic signals;

2) Impatience in waiting for traffic signals or other drivers or pedestrians;

3) Competition with other drivers for speed or preferred placement in lines; and

4) Punishing other drivers for their mistakes.

Some of the following suggestions regarding how to keep other drivers from becoming angry with you are adapted from the AAA website at: www.aaafts.org.

1. **Don't offend** other drivers by cutting them off, driving slowly in the left lane, tailgating, or using inappropriate gestures.

- If you are in the left lane and someone wants to pass, move over and let them by. You may be "in the right" because you are traveling at the speed limit, but you may also be putting yourself in danger by angering drivers behind you. It's a simple courtesy to move over and let other drivers by.

- Drivers get angry when they are followed too closely. Allow at least a two-second space between your car and the car ahead. (A "two-second space" means you can count "one-one thousand, two-one thousand" between the time the back of a car in front of you passes a stationary object, and the time the front of your car reaches the same spot.) If you think another car is driving too slowly and you are unable to pass, pull back and allow more space, not less. If you feel you are being followed too closely, signal and pull over to allow the other driver to go by.

- Nothing makes another driver angrier than an obscene gesture! Keep your hands and all of your fingers on the wheel! Avoid making any gestures that might anger another driver.

2. **Don't engage** in confrontations. Angry people do things they may later regret. If you are tempted to retaliate against another driver, think: "Would I want to fly in an airplane with a pilot who acts like this?" Think about what kind of an accident your angry actions could cause.

- Stay away from drivers who may want a fight. Slow down and give the angry driver a lot of room. Do not pull off to the side of the road and try to settle things, "man to man" or "woman to woman."

Verbal encounters can turn violent.

- Just as forest rangers advise you not to look into the eyes of a charging bear, don't make eye contact with another driver who is acting angrily with you. Eye contact can be taken as a personal challenge. Once things get personal, the situation can get out of hand quickly!

- If you believe that an angry driver is following you or is trying to pick a fight, get help. If you have a cellular phone, use it to call the police. Otherwise, drive to a place where there are people around, such as a police station, convenience store, shopping center, or even a hospital. Use your horn to get attention. This will usually discourage an aggressor. Do not get out of your car or go home alone until the aggressor quits following you.

Suggestions that will help prevent teens (and adults) from becoming angry with other drivers are:

1. **Leave early!** Individuals with AD/HD are notorious for being late and then trying to make up lost time on the road. One of the hallmark characteristics of individuals with AD/HD is that they often lose things that are necessary for the task at hand. In driving, those things that are lost are typically the keys to the vehicle or the billfold containing the license! Charging around the house in a frantic hunt for these lost items before driving is emotionally distracting. Parents need to help teens establish specific places for those important items when they are not used. It may be that the keys and wallet would be kept in a special bowl near the back door, or that a special key hanger would be installed by the door leading to the garage. It's a good idea to have a spare set of keys tucked away in case the keys given to the teen are gone forever!

   Teens with AD/HD need to learn to start early and allow plenty of time for their trips. AAA suggests that instead of trying to "make good time," drivers should try to "make time good." Listen to soothing music. Practice relaxation techniques such as deep breathing. You'll arrive safely and much calmer.

2. **Put yourself in the other driver's shoes.** Someone speeding and constantly changing lanes may be a volunteer fireman or a physician rushing to a hospital. Whatever the reason, don't make it your problem. Remain calm and drive defensively.

Watch for high-risk road rage behaviors in your teen. If you observe these behaviors, then your teen should be enrolled in an anger management treatment program and not be allowed to continue driving until the anger is under control. Your physician or psychologist should be able to help you find an appropriate anger management treatment program if you have trouble locating one. Earning the right to drive can be a powerful incentive for a teen to complete an anger control treatment program.

Parent and Teen Activity:

The American Automobile Association (AAA) Foundation offers a Driver Stress Profile, a test to measure one's hostility on the road, on its website. The website address is: www.aaafoundation.org/Text/ aggressive.cfm. Parents as well as teens can learn about their own tendencies toward aggressive driving. While you are at this website, you'll want to look at other safe driving tips.

Addressing Alcohol or Substance Abuse Issues

Recent studies of AD/HD and alcohol/substance abuse have shown that unmedicated youth with AD/HD, especially those with coexisting Conduct Disorder, may be more likely than those taking medication to become involved in serious alcohol and substance abuse. Parents need to give the message loud and clear, "Don't drink and drive." If your teen can't follow that rule, they should not be driving! Wise parents will take the keys away until these problems are resolved through appropriate treatment and before the teen is injured or injures another person.

If your teen is drinking alcohol or abusing substances and then driving, it is your parental responsibility to immediately suspend all driving privileges. Save yourself and others in the community a lot of grief — buy a new pair of walking shoes for the teen or pump up the bicycle tires! If your teen has become dependent upon either alcohol or substances, professional help is needed. The teen must earn the privilege of driving by demonstrating responsible behavior. Find help for your child and treat the abuse problems aggressively. Earning the privilege to learn to drive can also be used as a strong incentive for successful completion of and adherence to an alcohol or substance abuse treatment program.

Consequences For Alcohol, Inhalant, or Substance Use

- Assign **serious** consequences in the driving contract for alcohol/substance abuse. At a minimum, no less than the surrender of the driver's license for a specified period of time is appropriate.

- Parents should keep both the teen's keys and license in their possession until the alcohol and/or substance abuse issues are resolved.

- Restore driving privileges one step at a time. Do not allow full, unrestricted driving privileges until you are confident the teen is no longer using alcohol or substances.

Teens with previous alcohol or substance abuse offenses need to be carefully monitored for appropriate driving behaviors. Parents can regularly conduct unannounced inspections of the teen's car for signs of alcohol or substance abuse. Because of peer pressure involved in alcohol/substance abuse, specific preventative measures may need to be added to the driving contract, such as restricting driving times, limiting the social circle of the teen, and enforcing a no passenger rule. Ignoring the behavior or denying that this behavior exists is placing the teen's life, and possibly the lives of other people, in great danger.

Tragedy Turned to Future Hope

Edward Callister was an engaging young man and dedicated to playing football. He also suffered from AD/HD. Unfortunately, Edward used drugs and alcohol to ease his frustrations and was treated for his addiction on four separate occasions at various treatment centers. Edward died on April 22, 1997, from injuries suffered in a single-car accident.

The Edward G. Callister Foundation was established by Louis and Ellen Callister in honor of their son. The Callisters are dedicated to increasing public awareness of conditions that may lead to susceptibility to substance abuse in children and adults. Their foundation is committed to gaining a better understanding of addiction through research and education, and to providing assessment, referrals, and clinical services to those whose lives are affected by addiction. Through the foundation, they work to help other parents avoid the anguish of losing a child to addiction.

Resources for Alcohol and/or Substance Abuse

Remember that no single treatment is appropriate for everyone. Effective treatment may include a combination of individual psychotherapy, family counseling, and prescription medications. Some treatment options are more successful than others. Parents must become knowledgeable about addiction and about the various kinds of treatment that are available. Parents should do whatever it takes to support the teen's recovery and monitor successful completion of the treatment program *before* granting driving privileges.

A list of excellent resources follows for information about anger and driving, as well as alcohol and substance abuse.

Resources:

AAA Foundation for Traffic Safety, 1440 New York Ave., NW Suite 201, Washington, DC 20005. Telephone: 202-638-5944; FAX: 202-638-5943; Website: www.aaafts.org

Goodstat, A., and Parker, H. (1999). *"Substance Abuse in Adolescence."* 171-191. In Parker, H. (Ed.). *Put Yourself in Their Shoes: Understanding Teenagers with Attention Deficit Hyperactivity Disorder.* Plantation, FL: Specialty Press, Inc.

Larson, J. A. (1996). *Steering Clear of Highway Madness.* Inc. Wilsonville, OR: Book Partners.

Redford, W. (1993). *Anger Kills.* New York: Random House.

Some of the **organizations** that offer information about substance abuse are:

American Council for Drug Education. For written information call: 1-800-488-DRUG. For drug related problems, call: 1-800- 378-4435. Website: www.acde.org

Center for Substance Abuse Prevention. Website: www.samhsa.gov

Edward G. Callister Foundation Hotline Services: 1-801-587-HOPE or 801-587-4674. Written information or companion video documentary: 801-292-2632. Website: www.hopetoday.com For help in finding the right resources for you and your family, you may wish to contact the Callister Foundation, P.O. Box 540041, North Salt Lake, Utah 84054, 801-292-2632.

National Clearinghouse for Alcohol and Drug Information. 1-800-SAY- NOTO. Website: www.health.org

National Commission Against Drunk Driving.
Website: www.ncadd.com

National Council on Alcoholism and Drug Dependence.
1-212-206-6770. Website: www.ncadd.org

National Institute on Alcohol Abuse and Alcoholism.
Website: www.niaa.nih.org

Mothers Against Drunk Driving
1-214-744-6233. Website: www.madd.org

RID (Remove Intoxicated Drivers), National Office, PO Box 520,
Schenectady, NY 12301. Website: www.crisny.org
Includes information on teenage binge drinking and alcohol poisoning.

Students Against Destructive Decisions (formerly Students Against Drunk
Driving), PO Box 800, Marlborough, MA 01752, 1-877-SADD-INC.
Website: www.sadd.online.com

Step #3
Determine the maturity/driving readiness of your teen.

"Maturity is not the same as chronological age."
-Russell Barkley, Ph.D.

Parents should not be manipulated into believing that driving is a
teenager's right! A driver's license should not be thought of as "a rite of
passage" that is automatically bestowed on the teen's 15th or 16th birthday.
Parents have the power and the obligation to delay teen driving until their
teen's behaviors and attitudes toward driving are sufficiently mature.

Youth with AD/HD are often emotionally and functionally immature
when compared to peers of the same age. Teens with AD/HD, therefore,
may take significantly longer than other teens to develop good judgment and
a mature attitude toward driving. Dr. Russell Barkley and other researchers
working in the area of AD/HD have observed that individuals with AD/HD
typically function at a level about one-third less than their chronological age
in their ability to inhibit behavior. For example, a 16-year-old with severe
AD/HD may be unable to inhibit inappropriate behaviors and may act much
more like a 10 or 11-year-old without AD/HD. Would you encourage a 10 or
11-year-old to drive on busy streets or highways?

Teens who have explosive tempers, are uncooperative in school, or
have difficulty meeting their present responsibilities are not ready to drive.

A teen must understand that driving is a privilege and not a right. If important home and school responsibilities are not assumed without constant reminders, arguing, or threats, what evidence do you have that driving responsibilities will be handled differently? Don't be afraid to delay driving until your teen has matured enough to exhibit more responsible behavior and emotional control. Listen to your teen. You will get messages that will help you determine your teen's maturity level.

Is Your Teen Able to Separate Fantasy from Reality?

Many parents of teens with AD/HD have expressed concern about their teen's approach to learning how to drive a real car after years of watching car chases on television and racing cars on video games. Video games simulate fast driving or racing, without teaching the reality of what can happen to those who exceed the speed limit. When a car crashes on a video game, the player can merely push the reset button and get a new car! Car chases and races in movies are depicted as extremely exciting, with drivers often shown as heroes. Those unrealistic media presentations may lead impulsive, risk-taking teens to speed in their cars without fear of consequence.

Teens often think that accidents and fatal crashes cannot happen to them. Parents need to discuss with their child the reality of actual car accidents in contrast to video driving games and car chases shown in the movies **before** allowing the teen to get behind the wheel. Until your teen can make the distinction between fantasy and reality and can discuss safe driving behaviors realistically, your teen should not be driving a real motor vehicle. Help teens to understand that they are vulnerable! If they don't get the message that teen drivers can kill or be killed, they are simply not emotionally mature enough to learn how to drive.

It's also good for parents to think about how the teen's learning to drive will impact their younger siblings.

Justin had just finished his driving lesson. His younger brother, Todd, was eleven years old, has AD/HD, and was present during the lesson. Having watched his older brother, he decided that he, too, could drive the family car. He backed the car out of the driveway and then decided he had better put the car back. He pulled into the garage, but instead of applying the brakes, he gave it the gas! The car finally stopped after the family freezer was smashed through an interior wall of the home. In addition to the costs of repairing the car and getting a new freezer, an expensive home remodeling job was required. The child and family were temporarily traumatized but, thankfully, there were no serious physical injuries.

Commentary Driving

In his book, *Learning to Drive*, Warren Quensel suggests "commentary driving", a method for checking out how well a driver or passenger can identify all the events happening around the vehicle. As you drive, simply report aloud the traffic picture as it unfolds, making comments about whatever you see in the traffic scene around you. This should include what you see in front of your vehicle, to the sides, and in your mirrors.

For example, your commentary while driving through an intersection could be, "Open intersection... Speed limit is 35, and my speed is 37... I need to slow down. The upcoming signal light is going to turn red soon. The walk light just flashed off. My lane must turn left. There is no turn on red. I must yield to the van. I will stop and wait for the next green light. When I turn, I will turn into the left lane. We will then be on the state highway, in a no passing zone."

Do this a few times to give your teen an opportunity to see what it is you are doing. Then ask your teen to do the commentary while you do the driving. This method is helpful as a teaching technique, and can provide an opportunity to spend some enjoyable time with your teen. Participating in commentary driving will force your teen to identify things quickly and in advance of your car. You will then have a better idea as to whether your teen is seeing events in time to take proper defensive actions. It will also give you a chance to compare observations and to consider your teen's maturity and readiness to learn how to drive.

Parents Must Give Written Permission for a Learner's Permit

Parents of teens under 18 years of age need to be reminded that teens cannot obtain a learner's permit or a driver's license anywhere in the United States without parental permission. Only after careful planning should parents provide signatory permission for their teen to obtain a learner's permit. When signing for a learner's permit, parents should be convinced that their teen can handle driving responsibilities safely and that they as parents are prepared to assume any financial, legal, and emotional costs that may result from their child's negligence.

It is also important to note that parents may withdraw their permission for a teen to drive at any time until the teen is 18 years old. Parents should use this option if teen driving behaviors spiral out of control. If permission is withdrawn, the teen will be required to start again with the learner's permit and retake the driver's tests once the parents choose to allow it. Withdrawal of parental permission to drive is a natural consequence for poor or unsafe driving behavior. Gaining permission to get a learner's permit can be used as a powerful incentive for a teen to improve behavior and become more interested in safety issues.

Visiting with other parents about their experiences leads safety-conscious parents to the conclusion that the best possible thing parents can do for children with AD/HD is to delay their trip to the Department of Motor Vehicles until they are emotionally and functionally mature. Do not let your child sit in the driver's seat just because a specific birthday has been celebrated.

References:

Barkley, R. (1998). *Attention Deficit Hyperactivity Disorder: A Handbook for Diagnosis and Treatment.* Second Edition. New York and London: Guilford Press.

Quensel, W.P. *Parent-Teen Manual for Learning to Drive: Practice Driving Lessons for the Family Car.* Safety Enterprises, 1010 South Summit, Bloomington, IL. 309/828-0906.

Step #4
Familiarize yourself and your teen
with your state's driving laws.

"Ignorance of the law is no excuse." Judge Gerald E. Rouse.

Statistics for traffic fatalities are often the justification used to pass legislation to create new laws that help to reduce traffic fatalities. It is important for teens and parents to understand the reasons for the laws that they are expected to obey.

State Driving Laws and Regulations Save Lives

States have found that regulations regarding beginning drivers can reduce teen driving accidents and keep more teenagers alive. Some of those regulations include graduated licensing laws; regulations on teen passengers in cars driven by teens; zero tolerance for blood alcohol levels; seat belt laws; and speed limits. A few states have license regulations concerning staying in school and preventative rules for suspension and revocation of teen drivers' licenses.

Graduated Licensing Laws

In an effort to reduce the numbers of teen deaths in motor vehicle crashes, graduated licensing for teenagers has been adopted in 39 states. Graduated licensing is a system for phasing in on-road driving, allowing beginners to get their initial experience under conditions that involve lower risk and introducing them in stages to more complex driving situations. Graduated licensing is an apprentice system that involves three stages. The first stage is a supervised learner's period, followed by an intermediate licensing phase that permits unsupervised driving in less risky situations only. Finally, an unrestricted, full privilege license becomes available as the teen demonstrates a safe driving record and reaches the age of 18 years.

Typical graduated licensing restrictions include:

- A learner's permit that requires an adult licensed driver to be with new drivers at all times when they drive;
- No passengers except the adult supervisor during the first months of beginning driving;
- No driving between midnight and 5:00 a.m.;
- No driving over 55 miles per hour; and
- No application for an unrestricted license until the teen is violation-free and accident-free for 12 months on the learner's permit.

Educate yourself and support meaningful graduated licensing efforts in your state. Don't allow yourself to be lulled into a false sense of security because you think your state has graduated licensing. Be alert to the fact that there are numerous variations of graduated licensing which greatly impact teen driving outcomes. For example, some states put restrictions on the numbers of passengers teen drivers may have in the car — other states have no such restrictions. Some states restrict late-night driving times for teens while other states do not.

Parents and teens can find specific information about graduated licensing in their state driver's manual. Go to the American Automobile Association (AAA) website to compare your state's regulations with other states at www.aaa.com/news12LTLlictolearn/GDL.htm.

Your state's graduated licensing laws may not be as complete as you would wish them to be. Parents can institute their own graduated licensing requirements, however, through their own Teen Driving Contract, which will be discussed in detail in Steps #8 and #17.

Graduated licensing has been in effect in New Zealand and Canada for several years. Florida was the first state in the U.S. to enact comprehensive graduated licensing. Graduated licensing does reduce teen involvement in crashes, prevent injuries, and saves lives.

Illustration by Isaiah Amborsini

No Passengers for Beginning Drivers

When Amy first received her car, she promised her parents that she would not transport other kids and would drive a direct route to and from school. Her parents were called to an accident scene in a neighborhood where their daughter did not have permission to drive. Most likely, she had been distracted by her two teenage passengers. The inattentive driver missed noticing another driver backing out of his driveway and did not yield for him. The backing driver crashed into the passenger side of Amy's car, causing damage in the thousands of dollars. The car was repaired faster than the trust that had been lost between Amy and her parents.

Be aware that risks increase when your teen driver transports passengers without adults present. Don't assume your child will drive the same way with peers in the car as when you are present. A survey of 192 high-school-age drivers conducted by Farrow reported that dangerous driving behaviors (driving after drinking alcohol or using drugs, speeding, swerving, crossing the center line, purposely skidding, and running a red light) were strongly associated with the presence of peers in the teen's vehicle.

Another study reported in the Journal of the American Medical Association shows that the risk of fatal injury for a 16 or 17-year-old driver increases significantly with the number of passengers who are under 30 years of age, irrespective of the time of day or the gender of the driver. Teens driving with just one passenger increased their risk of death by 39% compared with teens driving without passengers. Two passengers increased the risk of fatal crash by 86%, and three passengers sent fatality risk rates soaring to over 182%! Knowing about these studies, does it really make any sense for parents to allow teens to have passengers in their car? Teens are certainly not safe being passengers of other teenage drivers either!

Zero Tolerance

Zero tolerance refers to state laws that provide for suspension of the driving privileges of any person under the age of 21 who drives after consuming alcohol. Like the name "zero tolerance" suggests, any trace of alcohol in a young persons system can result in a suspended driver's licence. The zero tolerance law provides that minors suspected of driving under the influence can have their driving privileges suspended even if they're not intoxicated at the 0.10 level.

Parents' Note: If your teenager is taking medication for an AD/HD condition or other disorders, ask your physician to specifically discuss the impact of the use of alcohol and its interaction with the medications the teen is taking. Private, frank, and honest conversations with their physicians are often more important to teens than hearing this information from a parent alone.

Seat Belt Laws

The first fatality of the year 2000 in Montana was a 16-year-old boy, killed when he rolled his car. He was not wearing a seat belt.

You can help your teen driver avoid death or a serious injury by insisting that they wear seat belts, even if the trip is just a block down the road! The greatest percentage of vehicle accidents occur within two miles of home. Responsible drivers use a seat belt and require that all their passengers use seat belts as well.

Lap/shoulder safety belts have been shown to be effective in reducing serious injury and saving lives, and are required by every state in the country. It's important for you and your teen to know and follow your state's specific seat belt laws. Some states require that only the driver and passenger in the front seat wear seat belts. Some states require that all passengers buckle up, regardless of where they are sitting. Studies reveal, however, that less than 40% of teen drivers use their seat belts. Death is a tragic unnecessary consequence when buckling up is so easy.

Air Bags

Air bags have demonstrated that they can save lives. They work best when everyone is buckled with both a lap and shoulder belt into their seats and children are properly restrained in the back seat. According to NHTSA figures, the combination of seat belts and air bags is estimated to be 75% effective in preventing serious head injuries and 66% effective in preventing serious chest injuries that are common in car crashes.

Children riding in the front seat can be seriously injured or killed when an air bag inflates in a crash. An air bag is not a soft, billowy pillow. To do its important job, an air bag comes out of the dashboard at up to 200 miles per hour. That is faster than the blink of an eye! The force of an air bag can hurt those who are sitting too close to the bag. Air bag deployment has been known to shatter the windshield of cars in accidents.

NHTSA makes several recommendations concerning the use of air bags, including: children 12-years-old and under should ride buckled up in a rear seat; infants in rear-facing child safety seats should never ride in the front seat of a vehicle with a passenger-side air bag; and small children should ride in a rear seat in child safety seats approved for their age and size. Questions concerning air bags can be directed to the Department of Transportation Auto Safety Hotline at 1-888-327-4236.

Parent and Teen Activity:

Discuss with your teen reasons why it's a good practice for all passengers in the car to wear seat belts. Even though you may not have an infant in the car, discuss the proper use of infant seats with your teenager. Teens should know where infant seats are placed and how they are to be belted in place. Be sure that your teen knows that small children are to be buckled into a child seat that is secured in the back seat.

Maximum Speed Limits

Craig had been arrested for driving 95 miles-per-hour in a 65 miles-per-hour zone. He had minor "fender benders" in the past, but this speeding violation was serious. He lost a number of points on his license and his insurance costs skyrocketed.

Police reports indicate that 36% of all 16-year-old drivers in fatal crashes were reportedly speeding or going too fast for road conditions. In a typical teen fatality accident, the teen's vehicle leaves the road and overturns or strikes an object like a tree or pole. Some adults may be surprised to know that the majority of teen fatalities occur in rural rather than urban areas. Teens have a tendency to drive faster in rural areas because they believe the wide-open spaces are safer.

Most parents are extremely worried about teen drinking and yet give little thought to excessive speeding. Excessive speed is more than twice as likely to be involved in 16-year-old fatalities than alcohol. Only 15% of all 16-year-old drivers killed in accidents in 1996 had blood alcohol concentrations above 0.10%. This compares with 32% of older teenage fatalities (17-19 years old), and 53% of fatal accidents for drivers 25-49 years old. It would appear that young teens are listening to "don't drink and drive" messages. Teens have shown that they can develop responsible, safe driving behaviors if they hear the message.

Teens need to get the message that "speed kills." Even in Montana where no numerical speed limits were posted on highways for a number of years, many drivers had a hard time deciding what speed was "reasonable and prudent." As a result, Montana saw an increase in highway fatalities related to excessive speed. Montana's laws have changed recently in response to those deaths. In the first year after specific speed limits were posted, highway deaths decreased by 7%. Messages in many gas stations throughout the state read, "Whoa, Mario! There is a speed limit in Montana. Drive safely!" Don't forget to give your teen the message about safe driving speeds! Be specific about your teen's speed limit. "Whoa" to the parent that believes inexperienced teenagers will be "reasonable and prudent." On the highway, 55 miles-per-hour is fast enough for any first-year driver!

Curfews

Some communities, such as Whitefish, Montana, still enforce 10:00 p.m. curfews for their teenagers, but most do not. Parents can insist on their own curfews, however, which can effectively prohibit unsupervised late-night driving. Late-night teen outings tend to be recreational and pose additional risk for vehicle accidents. Last year, 55% of all teen traffic deaths in the United States occurred on a Friday, Saturday, or Sunday. Of those crashes, 41% occurred after 9:00 p.m.

Parents need to be at home and awake to be able to monitor and enforce curfew compliance. Require that you are kept informed of your teen's driving activities. Where is your teen going? What route is being taken? Who is your teen meeting? What are they doing? When will your teen return? Be specific!

Radios, Tape Decks, CDs, Portable Televisions, Cell Phones, Fax Machines, Geographic Imaging System Computers

Illustration by Harley Addison

Electronic equipment in today's vehicles can be enjoyable and very helpful in keeping the driver alert and informed. However, the potential for distraction for any driver, and particularly for a new teen driver with AD/HD, can be deadly. Statistically, many states track a combination of miscellaneous distractions that have caused accidents. Some of these factors include dealing with children, lighting a cigarette, operating the radio, talking on the cell phone, reading, or sending a fax! Some states have begun regulating electronic equipment use, such as cell phones, while driving. Keep the drivers in your family safe. Work on keeping these distractions to a minimum. Don't allow electronic distraction while driving!

- There should be no music or radio interference/distractions during driving instruction time.

- When driving, the volume of audio equipment must be at a low enough level to allow the driver and the driving monitor/trainer to hear sounds that require action from the driver, such as emergency sirens, train whistles, or horns from other vehicles. Loud music in vehicles is distracting and can also cause long-term damage to an occupant's hearing. Parents should compare driving behaviors during different levels of music volume. If necessary, acceptable volume levels of the radio or stereo should be specified in the driving contract.

- It is not safe to hold a cellular phone to your ear while you are trying to drive. A research article published in 1997 in *The New England Journal of Medicine* concluded that collision risk is four times greater if you use a cellular phone while driving.

    Cellular phones are a good way of keeping in touch with your teen, but you should not allow the teen to use the cellular phone while driving. The cell phone should be turned off while the teen is driving alone in the car. Accepting an incoming call is just as dangerous as initiating a phone call while driving. In 1996 and 1998 a Japanese National Police Agency found that 42% of the phone-related accidents occurred while the driver was responding to a call. They found that drivers were startled or distracted by the ringing, dropping the phone, or turning back to pick up the phone.

    The New England Journal of Medicine reported that hands-free devices, often cited as a safety factor for cell phone use, involved approximately the same risks and accident rates as hand-held mobile phones.

- Try to avoid driving behind someone who is driving and using a cellular phone. Cellular phone users sometimes take risks while driving to take notes or look up phone numbers. If something should happen up ahead, being behind an inattentive driver can be a problem for the driver following.

- Trying to change radio stations, changing a tape or CD, watching a television show, or programming a geographic positioning system while driving distracts full attention from the driving tasks at hand.

- All loose items, in any area in the vehicle, need to be secured. These items will become projectiles if a sudden stop is required! Flying objects in the car can cause injury or be enough of a distraction to prevent timely, precise, and successful maneuvering of the vehicle to avoid collision.

State Laws May Differ

The state of Georgia has become proactive in trying to reduce the number of teens killed in that state by passing several thoughtful restrictions for drivers' licenses. Two interesting Georgia laws that certainly support driver responsibility are:

1. Stay-in-School Requirement (Effective January 1, 1998)

A. No one under age 18 shall be eligible for an instruction permit or a driver's license unless the applicant submits proof of being enrolled in school or having graduated from high school (including a GED), or has a parent or guardian's permission to withdraw from school.

B. An instruction permit or drivers license of anyone under the age of 18 will be suspended if the minor (1) drops out of school without parental permission; (2) misses ten consecutive days of school in a semester without an excuse; or, (3) is suspended from school for threatening or striking a teacher or school employee, possessing drugs or alcohol on school property, or possessing a weapon on school property. A license suspension of 90 days is mandatory for a suspension from school.

2. Suspensions and Revocations (Effective July 1, 1997)

Georgia drivers under age 21 will have their driver's license revoked for the following offenses:

- Hit-and-Run or Leaving the Scene of an Accident
- Racing or Eluding an Officer
- Reckless Driving
- Any Offense for which 4 or more Points are Assessed (offenses with less than 4 points are not cumulative and will not result in a license being revoked.)

- Purchasing or Attempting to Purchase an Alcoholic Beverage (a non-driving offense)
- Driving Under the Influence

Parents should take note of the Georgia law. It saves lives! Any teen who has offenses where four or more points are assigned for driving offenses must realize that their teen exhibits high-risk driving behaviors. Whether your state revokes the license or not, parents should consider whether or not they are willing to risk the health and life of their teen by ignoring their teen's driving record.

Parent and Teen Activity:

Secure two copies of your state's driver's handbook — one for you and one for your teen. Read the handbook carefully for information about regulations for the learner's permit, graduated licensing requirements, zero tolerance, curfews, passenger limitations, seat belt regulations, and basic driving laws of your state. Check to see if your state has a required number of hours of daytime or nighttime driving instruction before the unrestricted license is issued.

Encourage your teen to read your state's driver's manual and find the answers to the questions on the following worksheets. Discuss with your teen what was read and learned.

Since the tragic death of her daughter, Morgan, in a cell phone–related car accident, Patti Pena has been tirelessly campaigning for car phone/cell phone legislation. Her website is both a tribute to her daughter and a source of information about the subject of using cell phones while driving. Visit her website at www. geocities.com/morganleepena/. The Tappet Brothers, Click and Clack, of NPR radio fame, have started a national awareness campaign, "Drive Now....Talk Later." Visit their research section on cell phones at www.cartalk.cars.com

---

What Are Your State's Laws?

Question	Answer	Page #
1. What is the minimum age for getting a learner's permit in your state?		
2. Who is financially responsible for any damage resulting from a minor child operating a motor vehicle?		
3. How many hours of supervised driving are required before applying for a driver's license? How many hours will your parents require of you?		
4. If a license is "suspended," or "revoked" what does that mean?		
5. What kinds of circumstances can result in a license suspension or revocation?		
6. What is a "certified driving record"?		
7. How can a copy of a certified driver's record be obtained?		
8. How is a person's driving record used?		
9. What is a graduated driver's license?		
10. Does your state have a graduated licensing system? If it does, what are the requirements for each level?		
11. What is an "unrestricted" license?		
12. How old do you have to be to apply for a driver's license?		
13. What are the penalties for driving under the influence (DUI) of alcohol or other substances?		
14. What are the penalties for minor in possession?		
15. When involved in a crash, what happens to a driver who has no proof of insurance?		
16. What penalties exist for parents who allow children to use uninsured cars?		
17. What happens to your driver's license if you use your car in committing a crime?		

What Are Your State's Laws, continued...

Question	Answer	Page #
18. Does a license entitle you to drive a motorcycle or commercial motor vehicle?		
19. What telephone number can you call to report a suspected drunk driver?		
20. What fines apply for parking in a parking space for the handicapped?		
21. What is your responsibility if you are involved in an accident while driving?		
22. What kind of crime is it to leave the scene of an accident if you are involved in the accident?		
23. What penalties are common for those who "hit and run"?		
24. Who is responsible for licensing drivers in your state? What office do they hold?		
25. What kind of health problems can interfere with a driver's ability to drive safely?		
26. If convicted of a speeding violation in a work zone, what happens to the amount of the fine imposed?		
27. Are there any "stay in school" requirements for a driver's license in your state?		
28. Are teenagers allowed to donate organs for transplant programs in your state?		
Answers to the following questions will not be found in the state driver's manual.		
29. What is the location of your local licensing office?		
30. Who is your county sheriff? Location?		
31. Who is the Chief of Police in your city of residence? Where is this city official located?		
32. Who is the Driver Education teacher at your school?		

References:

Alm, H. and Nilsson, L. (1994). Changes in driver behaviors as a function of hands-free mobile telephones. *Accident Analysis and Prevention.* Vol. 26, (3), 441-451.

Alm, H. and Nilsson, L. (1995). The effects of a mobile telephone task on driver behavior in a car-following situation. *Accident Analysis and Prevention.* Vol. 27 (5), 707-715.

Chen, L., Baker, S. P., Braver, E. R., and Guohua, L. (March 22/29, 2000). Carrying Passengers as a Risk Factor for Crashes Fatal to 16- and 17-Year-Old Drivers. *Journal of the American Medical Association, Vol. 283, No. 12.*

Brookhuis, K. A., de Vries, G., and de Waard, D. (1991). The effects of mobile telephoning on driving performance. *Accident Analysis and Prevention,* Vol. 23 (4), 309-316.

Japanese National Police Agency. (August, 1996). Study of Injury-Producing Crashes During June, 1996. *Daily Automobile Newspaper.*

Redelmeier, D. A. and Tibshirani, R. J. (1997). Association between cellular-telephone calls and motor vehicle collisions. *The New England Journal of Medicine.* Vol. 336, (7), 453-458.

Step #5
Select driver education materials and plan the content of your teen's driving lessons.

There really is no one better to teach teens to drive than their parents. For years, parents serve as a child's chauffeur, driving to school, piano lessons, band practices, slumber parties, baseball games, doctor and dentist appointments, and to church. Over the years, parents invest thousands of hours of care, love, and worry into a child. Completely turning over the responsibility for teaching your teen an important life skill, such as driving, to someone else, just doesn't make sense! Learning to drive safely is truly a life or death issue for your teenager. Parents need to be involved with the teen and be responsible for guiding the process of learning how to drive safely. With some thought and planning, parents make excellent driving teachers! Take time to prepare for your teen's driving lessons. Plan the content of the lessons and plan how much time you will be spending with your teen to teach safe driving practices. Pre-drive the area where you are going to teach the lesson. Drive the lesson yourself before you instruct your teen. Note any hazards and special conditions about which you need to alert your teen. Develop a consistent terminology for the actions you want your teen to carry out and also for the conditions of the road that you want your teen to notice. Keep your lesson plan and copies of all observation forms in a folder in your vehicle. Having these materials ready will allow you and your teen to take advantage of unexpected opportunities for short lessons.

Three excellent resources that contain driving lessons for parents and teens are:

Safe Young Drivers was written by Phil Berardelli, who outlines ten basic skill-building lessons. Each lesson may need to be repeated numerous times until the teen has mastered control in order to advance to the next lesson. The format of this book is particularly helpful in that some sections are written especially for the parent giving driving instruction, and other sections contain special tips written especially for the teenager. The book features a spiral spine making it convenient for instruction.

Parent-Teen Manual for Learning to Drive: Practice Driving Lessons for the Family Car was written by Warren Quensel. Mr. Quensel, now retired, put over 25 years of experience as a state supervisor of driver education into this basic book that should be read by both the parent and the teen. At the end of each lesson, there are activities and coaching tips for the parent to follow.

Teaching Your Teens to Drive: A Partnership for Survival was developed by the American Automobile Association (AAA). The program includes an illustrated handbook, detailed parents guide, and either a live-action-video CD-ROM or video tape.

Parents will find suggestions in state drivers' manuals and various driver education resources for how much supervised driving practice time an average teen needs before applying for a license. These estimates vary from 25 to 100 hours! We know, from education studies, that individuals with AD/HD often need considerably more practice time to master academic and motor skills. Therefore, parents of teens with AD/HD should plan to spend no less than 100 hours and should not be surprised if it takes 150 to 200 hours of supervised driving (with a learner's permit) before consistent safe driving skills are acquired. It is important that the teen realizes that the goal is safe driving behaviors and skills rather than merely meeting the requirements of state law.

Teach Railroad Crossing Safety

Even though a motorist is more than 40 times more likely to die in an accident involving a train than with a collision with another motor vehicle, parents often forget to stress safety at railroad crossings. Operation Lifesaver is a nonprofit, nationwide public education program dedicated to reducing collisions, injuries, and fatalities at intersections where roadways meet railways. The key facts that parents and teens need to take away from the information at this website (www.oli.org) are:

- Each year, several hundred people are killed (399 in 1999) and over a thousand individuals are seriously injured in highway–rail grade crossing collisions.

- More people die in highway–rail grade crossing accidents in the United States each year than in all commercial and general aviation crashes combined.

- Nearly 50% of vehicle/train collisions occur at crossings with active warning devices (gates, lights, bells).

- Most collisions with trains occur within 25 miles of the motorist's home.

- Trains CANNOT stop quickly. (The average stopping distance for a freight train traveling 55 miles per hour is a mile or more.)

- Never drive around lowered crossing gates — it's illegal and deadly. If you think a cross arm is malfunctioning, do not drive across the track! Call the 1-800 number posted on or near the crossing signal or call your local law enforcement agency to report crossing guard malfunctions.

- Never race a train to the crossing — even if you tie, you will lose!

- If your vehicle stalls on the track, immediately get everyone out and far away from the tracks.

- Always expect a train to be on the track! Trains do not run regular schedules. Trains can be on the track at any time.

- Do not stop close to the track. Remember the train is three feet wider than the tracks on both sides! Leave plenty of room for the train to pass by and remember that you should stay well back from the tracks. If a driver hits you from behind while the train is going by, you may be pushed into the train if you are too close.

- Don't be fooled by an optical illusion. Trains are usually closer and going faster than you think. If you see a train approaching, wait for it to go by before you proceed across the tracks.

- At a multiple track crossing, wait for a train to pass and then watch for a second train on the other tracks. Trains can come from either direction!

Parent and Teen Activity:

Visit Operation Lifesaver on the Internet at www.oli.org. Check out the Highway-Rail Facts and discuss safety precautions that all drivers should take at railroad crossings. Look at all the examples of railroad crossing signs so that you and your teen are aware of the different kinds of rail crossing warning systems.

Drive to three railroad crossings that your teen will be crossing regularly. Stop near the crossing and look to see what distractions could keep a driver's attention from focusing on an oncoming train. Discuss those distractions and observe the crossing's warning system. Talk about the volume of radios and music in the car and how they can keep you from hearing a train whistle if they are being played too loudly. Teach the teen to shut off music and roll down the window so an approaching train can be heard. Drive across the track and turn around to see the same intersection from the opposite direction.

Discuss safe driving tips from the Operation Lifesaver site regarding railroad crossings and quiz your teen about how they will handle railroad crossings.

Resources for Driver Education Materials:

American Automobile Association (AAA). *Teaching Your Teens to Drive: A Partnership for Survival.* Instruction kit includes an illustrated handbook, detailed parents guide, and either a live-action-video CD-Rom or video tape. Contact the AAA Michigan Community Safety Services, 1 Auto Club Drive, Dearborn, MI 48126. 1-800-327-3444.

Berardelli, P. (1996). *Safe Young Drivers: A Guide for Parents and Teens.* EPM Publications, 1003 Turkey Run Road, McLean VA 22101. Website: www.safeyoungdrivers.com

Operation Lifesaver: instructional materials are available at website: www.oli.org Good information and driving tips are available on line. Contact information for each of the state directors of the Operation Lifesaver is also available.

Quensel, W. P. *Parent-Teen Manual for Learning to Drive: Practice Driving Lessons for the Family Car.* Safety Enterprises, 1010 South Summit, Bloomington, IL. 309/828-0906.

Step #6
Consider medication issues and driving safety.

Terry often forgot to take his medication, and when he forgot, he did really reckless or impulsive things with his car. One day, he decided to take his car across a field so he could save some time. This was not a four-wheel drive vehicle. Because the field was uneven and had several ditches running through it, he hit the bottom of the car and tore off the exhaust pipe. In the end, the car was hung up on the uneven soil and the teen had to get help to pull his car out of the field. His parents refused to repair the exhaust pipe, so he drove the terribly noisy car for some time before he was able to pay for the repairs.

The Use of Medications While Driving

Research has consistently shown that AD/HD behaviors can be significantly improved with medication use. Some of the known benefits of medication use include an increase in attention span and concentration, improved academic performance, and better interpersonal relationships. Using medication can help individuals to be able to more effectively and efficiently follow directions and to complete work tasks. Medication can provide a short-term decrease in an individual's hyperactivity level, non-compliance with rules, and disruptive or demanding behaviors. When the medication wears off, more intense and frequent problems with inattention, impulsivity, and irritability may be observed.

A recent study by Cepeda, Cepeda, and Kramer shows that non-medicated youth with AD/HD are three times slower when making decisions for switching between tasks than are their non-AD/HD counterparts. The study involved two experiments in a task-switching paradigm that measured executive control abilities. Participants had to process relevant information, discard distractions, and switch rapidly among different skills to make accurate decisions. The study also showed that medication dramatically improved the ability of youth with AD/HD "to react regardless of whether the task switch is frequent and predictable or infrequent and unpredictable. When medicated, the reaction time of individuals with AD/HD was the same as the control group." Kramer said, "When these kids are teenagers and go out to drive a car, a hundred milliseconds can become quite important to their safety if they have to swerve or apply the brakes to avoid an accident."

Distinguish between Medication Facts and Fiction

Parents and teens need to understand clearly when medication use is needed and when it is not. Parents and teens also need to understand what medications can do and what they cannot do. They need to be educated about medications that have been prescribed, and to monitor their effective-ness.

From time to time, parents will be approached by well-meaning individuals who are trying to sell alternatives to medication. Sometimes these alternatives are promoted as "cures" for AD/HD behaviors. Ingersoll and Goldstein suggest that parents considering other treatments that have not been validated through research be advised of the following warning signs:

- Overstatement and exaggerated claims for certain treatments are red flags. Parents should be suspicious of any product or treatment that is described as "astonishing," "miraculous," or "an amazing breakthrough". Legitimate medication and mental health professionals do not use words like these, nor do they boast of their success in treating huge numbers of patients.

- Parents should be advised to be suspicious, too, of any therapy that claims to treat a wide variety of ailments. Common sense tells us that the more grandiose the claim, the less likely it is there is any real merit behind it.

- Parents should not rely on testimonials from people who say they have been helped by the product or treatment. First, legitimate medical and mental health professionals do not solicit testimonials from their patients. Second, testimonials are not substitutes for evidence. Third, patient enthusiasm is also not a substitute for scientific evidence. Testimonials in no way prove effectiveness. Choosing treatments for your child's attention and impulse problems is not like choosing a mechanic for your car.

- Parents should request printed information about a treatment they are considering. They should be wary if the bulk of this information is published by a particular practitioner or by a group whose sole purpose is to promote that treatment.

Medication Concerns

There has been a lot of publicity, both positive and negative, about using medications to treat AD/HD. Unfortunately, much of the debate has centered around the use of one medication, methylphenidate, commonly referred to by the brand name Ritalin™. Ritalin™ is only one of a number of medications that have been shown to be beneficial in the treatment of AD/HD. Media hype and misinformation have, unfortunately, caused some parents and teens to reject needed medical treatment for AD/HD.

It is very important to understand the risks associated with not treating AD/HD. Untreated AD/HD increases the risk of school failure, suspension, expulsion, and personal injury accidents. Long term outcome studies show that untreated AD/HD is associated with increased rates of substance abuse, teen pregnancy, delinquent behavior, and suicide. AD/HD is not a minor childhood disorder that will be outgrown. Treating AD/HD is a quality of life issue. Ultimately, medication usage is a personal choice that should be made with full understanding of the issues involved.

Medications Commonly Used for AD/HD

Medications commonly used to treat AD/HD are divided into four classifications: stimulants, antidepressants, mood stabilizers, and antihypertensives. Recently, new medication options have been made available.

Stimulant Medications
- Ritalin ™ (methylphenidate)
- Dexedrine ™ (dextroamphetamine)
- Adderall ™ (dextroamphetamine and amphetamine)
- Cylert ™ (magnesium pemoline)
- Metadate ™ (8 hour methylphenidate)
- Concerta ™ (10 hour methylphenidate)

Antidepressant Medications
- Tricyclics Norpramin ™ (desipramine)
- Pamelor ™ or Vivactyl ™ (nortryptyline)
- Tofranil ™ (imipramine)

SSRIs - Selective Serotonin Re-uptake Inhibitors
- Paxil ™ (paroxetine)
- Prozac ™ (fluoxetine)
- Zoloft ™ (sertraline)

Other Antidepressants
- Anafranil ™ (clomipramine)
- Buspar ™ (buspirone)
- Effexor ™ (venlafaxine)
- Welbutrin ™ (buproprion)

Antihypertensives
- Catapres ™ (clonidine)
- Tenex ™ (guanfacine)

Mood Stabilizers
- Depakote ™ (valproic acid)
- Lithionate ™ (lithium carbonate)

Finding the right medication, dosage, and schedule takes time and effort. Because of the added risks associated with the driving behaviors of teens with AD/HD and coexisting disorders, driving should be considered within the context of the overall medical treatment plan. Parents can be helpful in determining when medication is needed by observing their teen's driving skills, reaction time, and attitudes toward safety at different times throughout the day, when medication varies in effectiveness. Determine if there are any medication side effects, such as drowsiness, that could cause safety concerns. Both parents and teens should become knowledgeable about the medications that they are using to help control AD/HD or other coexisting conditions.

The following chart is reprinted with permission: Parker, H. (2000) *Problem Solver Guide for Students with AD/HD*, page 132.

Medication Chart to Treat AD/HD*

*Dose varies from individual to individual. Information presented here does not include all medications for AD/HD and is not intended to replace the advice of a physician.

DRUG	DOSING	COMMON SIDE EFFECTS	DURATION OF BEHAVIORAL EFFECTS	PROS	PRECAUTIONS
RITALIN® Methylphenidate Tablets 5 mg 10 mg 20 mg	Start with morning dose of 5 mg/day and increase up to 0.3-0.7 mg/kg of body weight. 2.5-60 mg/day*	Insomnia, decreased appetite, weight loss, headache, irritability, stomachache	3-4 Hours	Works quickly (within 30-60 minutes); effective in about 50 % of adult patients; good safety record.	Use cautiously in patients with marked anxiety, motor tics, or with a family history of Tourette syndrome.
RITALIN-SR® Methylphenidate Tablets 20 mg	Start with morning dose of 20 mg and increase up to 0.3-0.7 mg/kg of body weight. Up to 60 mg/day*	Insomnia, decreased appetite, weight loss, headache, irritability, stomachache	About 7 Hours	Particularly useful for adolescents and adults to avoid needing a noon time dose; good safety record.	Use cautiously in patients with marked anxiety, motor tics or with a family history of Tourette syndrome.
CONCERTA® Methylphenidate Tablets 18 mg 36 mg	Once a day dosing in morning Start with 18 mg and increase up to 54 mg.	Insomnia, decreased appetite, weight loss, headache, irritability, stomachache	About 12 Hours	Works quickly (within 30-60 minutes); avoid needing a noon time or afternoon dose.	Use cautiously in patients with marked anxiety, motor tics or with a family history of Tourette syndrome.
DEXEDRINE® Dextroamphetamine Tablets Spansules 5 mg 5 mg 10 mg	Start with morning dose of 5 mg/day increase up to 0.3-0.7 mg/kg of body weight. Give in divided doses 2-3 times/day. 2.5-40 mg/day*	Insomnia, decreased appetite, weight loss, headache, irritability, stomachache	3-4 Hours (tablets) 8-10 Hours (spansules)	Works quickly (within 30-60 minutes); may avoid noon time dose in spansule form; good safety record.	Use cautiously in patients with marked anxiety, motor tics or with a family history of Tourette syndrome.
ADDERALL® Mixed salts of a single-entity amphetamine Tablets 5 mg 10 mg 20 mg 30 mg	Start with a morning dose of 2.5 mg for 3-5 years olds. For 6 and older, start with 5 mg once or twice daily.	Insomnia, decreased appetite, weight loss, headache, irritability, stomachache	4-6 Hours	Works quickly (within 30-60 minutes); action may last somewhat longer than other standard stimulants.	Use cautiously in patients with marked anxiety, motor tics or with a family history of Tourette syndrome.
TOFRANIL® Imipramine Hydrochloride Tablets 10 mg 25 mg 50 mg	Start with dose of 25 mg in evening and increase 25 mg every 3-5 days as needed. Given in single or divided doses, morning & evening. 25-150 mg/day*	Dry mouth, decreased appetite, dizziness, mild tachycardia, headache, stomachache, constipation	12-24 Hours	Helpful for ADD patients with comorbid depression or anxiety; lasts throughout the day.	May take 2-4 weeks for clinical response; to detect pre-existing cardiac defect a baseline ECG may be recommended. Discontinue gradually.
NORPRAMIN® Desipramine Hydrochloride 10 mg 75 mg 25 mg 100 mg 50 mg 150 mg	Start with dose of 25 mg in evening and increase 25 mg every 3-5 days as needed. Given in single or divided doses, morning & evening. 25-150 mg/day*	Dry mouth, decreased appetite, headache, dizziness, constipation, mild tachycardia	12-24 Hours	Helpful for ADD patients with comorbid depression or anxiety; lasts throughout the day.	May take 2-4 weeks for clinical response; to detect pre-existing cardiac defect a baseline ECG may be recommended. Discontinue gradually.
CLONIDINE® Catapres Tablets Patches .1 mg TTS-1 .2 mg TTS-2 .3 mg TTS-3	Start with dose of of .025-.05 mg in evening and increase by similar dose every 3-7 days as needed. Given in divided doses 3-4 times/day. 0.15-3 mg/day*	Sleepiness, hypotension, dizziness, nausea, dry mouth, localized skin reactions with patch.	3-6 Hours (oral form) 5 days (skin patch)	Helpful for AD/HD patients with comorbid tic disorder or severe hyperactivity and / or aggression	Sudden discontinuation could result in rebound hypertension; to avoid daytime tiredness starting dose given at bedtime and increased slowly.

Medication and Driving Observation Forms

A sample observation form has been provided at the end of Step #6. Make multiple copies of this observation form and use one each time you drive with your teen. Observe and record the characteristics of AD/HD as they relate to driving behaviors. Note the good, the bad, and the ugly! Record whether your teen is medicated or not medicated, and whether the medication is at its effective peak or is wearing off. Critically observe your teen's driving behaviors (steering, speed, awareness of the road, stopping, yielding, and attention to the driving environment), and compare the observations you make over time. This should be done regularly, and you should continue observing your teen even after licensing occurs.

Don't try to "grade" your teen while you are driving, but fill in the observation form immediately after each session. Give your undivided attention to the task at hand while you are giving the driving lesson. Give appropriate verbal feedback and encouragement to your teen during the driving season. Because drivers with AD/HD often exhibit high-risk behaviors, be ready to discontinue the driving session if things do not go well. You may find it necessary to conduct medicated and unmedicated driving comparisons in a vacant parking lot due to the added risk associated with some individuals when driving without the benefit of their medication.

Wait until the driving lesson is finished and you are both somewhat relaxed before going through the written evaluation form with your teen. Use this form to help you and the teen see the variable driving patterns between the medicated and unmedicated observations. It is important for parents to fill out these forms and keep them in a file so that patterns in driving behavior can be charted. Decide where the teen is doing well and look at when and where improvement is needed.

Look for emerging patterns of skill, attitude, or behavior in the teen's driving. Look for times that the teen's strengths are noted and also the times when driving mistakes are more common. For example, if there are more driving mistakes made between the hours of 6:00 p.m. and 7:00 p.m., and this time coincides with the wearing off of medication benefits, this may point out a need to visit with a physician to extend medication schedules to cover these driving times. Late afternoon, evening, or night driving may require a supplemental dosage of medication. Be aware that your teen may experience difficulty getting to sleep when taking medications later in the day. Perhaps a change in the kind of medication, or using a long-acting form of the medication could be of benefit.

Take the forms to your teen's medical appointments and discuss your observations and concerns with the treating physician. Sometimes medication side effects or changes in the medication's effectiveness take place during adolescence. Discuss options with the treating physician that may include a change in type of medication, dosage, and/or times medication may be taken. Watch for signs of drowsiness or problems with medication tolerance while driving. After observations and medication adjustments are made, you may continue to notice patterns in the teen's driving behaviors that will tell you that during certain times of the day it is not safe for your teen to drive. Your teen should not be allowed to drive during those times. It is the parent's responsibility to restrict the teen's driving to those times when the teen functions well.

Parent and Teen Activity:

Use the observation forms when your teen is driving in an unmedicated condition and at times when your teen is medicated. Determine if the medications offer improved behaviors or improved driving skills. If medications make observable improvements in driving behaviors, parents should require the use of medication as a condition of learning how to drive.

Parents and teens need to discuss where extra medications will be kept so that the teen will be able to comply with the prescribed medication schedule when away from home. If a key chain with a medication compartment is selected as an option for having medications available, selection and purchase of the key chain should be done before the teen is allowed to apply for the driver's license. Keep an empty, labeled container for the medication in the glove compartment to prevent accusations that the medication is an illegal drug.

Visit www.whitefishconsultants.com for an example of a medication key chain. Parents and teens should consult with their physician to determine if long-acting medications would be more appropriate for management of their symptoms during driving time.

Teens and parents should become knowledgeable about the many medication options available for treating AD/HD and coexisting disorders. Select reputable resources such as those listed at the end of this section. Read about the different kinds of medication used for AD/HD and coexisting disorders and become familiar with their predicted benefits and side effects.

Compliance with Medication Schedules

In order to be a safe driver, teens with AD/HD and other high-risk behaviors must acknowledge that they have a disorder that may impact their driving skills. When professional race car drivers are interviewed after winning their races, they often comment that their success behind the wheel is because of their ability to concentrate. In order to be a safe driver, all drivers need to concentrate and avoid distractions. Most teens with AD/HD need the benefit of medication to do so. Because parents cannot be expected to follow their teens around to insure medication compliance, teens have to be responsible enough to administer their own medications in order to reduce the risk of vehicle accidents.

People with AD/HD are often forgetful. Consequently, failure to maintain a necessary supply of medication may become a problem. Brainstorm with your teen to find an agreeable solution to this problem. You may wish to store a small supply of medication in the glove compartment. It is best to keep your medication in a properly labeled medication container so that there is no question about the legitimacy of having the medication. Key rings that have a medication holder attached may enable your teen to conveniently carry extra medications while they will be driving.

Earning the right to learn to drive can be used as a powerful incentive for better compliance with medication schedules and for more mature parent–teen interactions about medication issues. Parent's permission to drive a family vehicle can be contingent upon the teen's medication compliance. Compliance with a medication schedule can also be one of the items addressed through the teen driving contract.

Illustration by Adam McCafferty

Driving Observation Form

Driver's Name _____

Person Observing _____

Date _____

Time of Day _____ (Circle One) a.m./p.m.

Time of Last Medication _____ a.m./p.m.

Amount of Medication _____

Observed Behaviors or Skills	Satisfactory	Unsatisfactory	Comments/Suggestions
Driver Attitude:			
1. Attentive and Focused			
2. Distractible			
3. Impulsive			
4. Cooperative			
5. Careful			
6. Communicates Properly			
7. Respects Passengers			
8. Respects Other Drivers			
9. Is Safety Conscious			
Pre-Driving Awareness:			
1. Checks Tires			
2. Cleans Windows			
3. Checks Car Gauges			
4. Uses Seat belts			
5. Checks Mirror Position			
6. Adjusts Driver's Seat			
7. Adjusts Headrest			
8. Adjusts Steering Wheel			
9. Scans for Hazards			

Observed Behaviors or Skills	Satisfactory	Unsatisfactory	Comments/Suggestions
Driving Skills:			
1. Starting the Car			
2. Smooth Shifting			
3. Even, Smooth Acceleration			
4. Even, Smooth Braking			
5. Driveway Turnabout			
6. Entry into Traffic			
7. Steering Forward			
8. Steering on Turns - Smooth			
9. Left Turns, Right Turns			
10. Using Signals Properly			
11. Using Mirrors Properly			
12. Yielding Properly to Cars			
13. Proper Lane Changes			
14. Yielding to Pedestrians			
15. Steering Backward			
16. Speed Control			
17. Following Distance			
18. Passing			
19. Pulling Out of Traffic			
20. Starting/Stopping on Hill			
21. Angle Parking			
22. Parking Uphill			
23. Parking Downhill			
24. Parallel Parking			
25. U-Turns			
26. 3 - Point Turn About			
27. Entering Expressway			
28. Exiting Expressway			
29. Proper Shut Down			
Appropriate Parking			
Puts Car in Park			
Emergency Brake			
Turns Off Motor			
Removes Belongings			
30. Exits Car Safely			

Parent and Teen Activity:

If it is determined that your teen performs driving tasks better when medicated, as compared to driving without medication, parents should require the use of medications when the teen drives. Be aware, however, that if the teen is required to give a urine sample, the use of those same, very helpful medications may cause law enforcement officials to believe that your teen is abusing drugs. The residue of stimulant medications will show in the sample and may cause the teen to "fail" screening by testing positive for drug use. This can cause legal difficulties in addition to any driving violation for which the teen was stopped.

Ask your physician to write a letter on their official letterhead stating that the medications that were prescribed for AD/HD are safe to use while driving. Your teen should read the letter from the physician, place it in the Emergency Packet (described later), and be prepared to supply law enforcement officers with the letter if the need should ever arise. This letter will help to explain why a certain element is found in any urine sample, but will not excuse the teen's illegal driving behavior. Even though this letter is provided to law enforcement officials, all the circumstances of the situation that brought the teenager to the attention of law enforcement officials will be taken into consideration. If it is determined that your teen is an unsafe driver or is guilty of using other drugs or alcohol while driving, then your teen will face the consequences the same as any other licensed driver.

An example of a physician's letter follows. It is provided as a suggested guide for the minimum information that should be included. Your physician may wish to add more information.

Physician's Letter

I. M. Concerned, M.D.
2700 Slow Down Lane
No Joke, MT 59000

Current Date

To Whom It May Concern:

(Patient's Name) is a patient in my practice and is being treated and monitored for Attention Deficit/ Hyperactivity Disorder (AD/HD). The treatment program includes the use of (name the specific medication). This medication can be safely used while operating a motor vehicle.

If a situation arises that should require additional information about this medication, or (Patient's Name)'s treatment plan, please call me at (area code - phone number).

Respectfully,

I. M. Concerned, M.D.

I. M. Concerned, M.D.

References:

Anastropoulos, A. D. (Aug. 2000). The MTA Study and Parent Training in Managing ADHD. *ADHD Report, Vol.* 8, No. 4, 7-9.

Ingersoll, B. and Goldstein, S. (1993). *Attention deficit disorder and learning disabilities: Realities, myths and controversial treatments.* New York: Wiley.

Parker, H. C. (2000). *Problem Solver Guide for Students with ADHD.* Plantation, FL: Specialty Press.

Pelham, W. E., Jr. (Aug. 2000). The NIMH Multimodal Treatment of ADHD (MTA) Study. *ADHD Report,* Vol. 8, No. 4, 9-13.

The MTA Cooperative Group (1999). A 14-month randomized clinical trial of treatment strategies for attention-deficit/hyperactivity disorder. *Archives of General Psychiatry,* 56, 1073-1086.

Wilens, T. E. (1999). *Straight Talk About Psychiatric Medications for Kids.* New York: Guilford Press.

Zeigler Dendy, C. A. (2000). *Teaching Teens with ADD and ADHD: A Quick Reference Guide for Teachers and Parents.* Bethesda, MD: Woodbine House.

Step #7
Establish an incentive system for teens to earn time to practice driving.

"Teens must understand that driving is a privilege that they should earn." Rae Hemphill

Experienced parents of teens with AD/HD often remark that using driving privileges as an incentive has improved homework compliance, medication compliance, grades, and cooperation with family and school rules. In fact, some parents of teens with AD/HD have indicated that the years during which the teen learned to drive were some of the best years they had with their teen. Teenagers need to earn the privilege of learning to drive by demonstrating responsible behavior first! Driving is a powerful incentive to encourage everyday behaviors to change!

Parents can design a system (often called a Home Token System, Credit System, or Token Economy) that allows teens to earn driving lesson time for every increment of appropriate behavior demonstrated at home and at school. For example, if medications have been prescribed for AD/HD or coexisting conditions, parents can require medication compliance before they consider allowing the teen to drive. Teens can earn driving privileges by taking their medications as prescribed. The incentive system should start before the learner's permit is secured so that when you get the permit, your teen has some time earned to "cash in" for their first lesson.

No matter which system you choose, there are common aspects involved in each. Basically, such a system is a contract between the teen and parents, stating that if the teen behaves in certain ways, the parents agree to provide certain rewards and/or privileges. These systems are often successful in promoting good behaviors because they:

- Clearly communicate expected/acceptable behaviors;
- Provide motivation or encouragement for the teen to want to perform well; and
- Visually document progress toward goals, by providing a chart for the teen to see advancement as parents track progress.

It takes time to set up such a system because parents need to think through and write out their expectations for the teen's behavior. They should also determine what they will do in response to the teen's behavior–both for rewards for desired behaviors and for consequences for behaviors that do not measure up to parental expectations. In the process, parents and teens will identify behaviors that are not productive and need to be stopped, as well as behaviors that are positive and need to be increased. Point values will be assigned to each. A chart is constructed reflecting these behaviors and then the teen's behavior is monitored. When good behaviors are displayed, the points add up. If unacceptable behaviors are observed, points are deducted. At the end of a specific time (usually a week), points are tallied and special rewards or privileges are given.

These token systems are discussed extensively in the following books that parents of AD/HD children may already have (or want to have) on their bookshelves.

Barkley, R. (1995). *Taking Charge of AD/HD.* Guilford Press.

Parker, H. (1999). *Put Yourself In Their Shoes; Understanding Teenagers with Attention Deficit Hyperactivity Disorder.* (Chapter 11: Using a Home Token Economy for Behavior Change.) Plantation, FL: Specialty Press.

If these systems seem to be too difficult for you and your teen to work out on your own, work with a school counselor, a psychologist, or a social

Sample Chart for Earning Driving Privileges

Point-Earning Behaviors:	Possible Points	M	Tu	W	Th	Fr	Sat	Sun
1. Dresses for school by __a.m.	5							
2. Has good attitude	20							
3. Makes eye contact	10							
4. Takes medicine promptly	15							
5. Takes complete phone messages	5							
6. Participates with family	20							
7. Washes car	15							
8. Extra points earned								
Total Points Earned								
Point-Deducting Behaviors:	**Possible Points**	**M**	**Tu**	**W**	**Th**	**Fr**	**Sat**	**Sun**
1. Argues with parents	10							
2. Leaves without permission	10							
3. Swears or yells in house.	10							
4. Doesn't study or do homework	20							
5. Refuses to take medication	15							
6. Stays out past curfew	20							
7. Lies to parents	20							
8. Other Penalty								
Total Points Deducted								
Rewards:	**Needed Points**	**M**	**Tu**	**W**	**Th**	**Fr**	**Sat**	**Sun**
1. Half-hour driving lesson	30							
2. Tickets to movie	50							
3. Can invite a friend to sleep over	40							
4. Order a pizza	50							
5. Can choose a family activity	20							
6. Extra 1/2 hour on curfew time	40							
7. Extra driving time	20							
Total Points Earned								
Total Points Deducted								
Total Points Cashed In								
Total Points Banked								
Week of								

worker to help you through the process. The token system can address a wide range of behaviors. You will see similarities between the token system and the teen driving contact, which follows in the next step.

A sample is included of a chart that you may wish to use after you have identified target behaviors for your teen on page 88. This chart was adapted from a similar chart presented by Dr. Harvey Parker's book, *Put Yourself in Their Shoes*, p. 103.

Step #8
Discuss safe driving expectations with your teen and create a teen driving contract which outlines important agreements to be honored during the time the teen is driving with a learner's permit.

"It has often been said that parents should give their children roots and wings. Somehow, as children become teenagers, they expect those wings to have four tires attached to them."
-Joshua Leblang, Ed.S., LCPC

The first thing parents should do is to talk about the ultimate risk they are taking by allowing their child to drive. Discuss the fact that there is a very real risk that the teen could be seriously injured or killed. Firmly resolve to do all you can as a parent to prevent this from happening. The teen should also pledge to do their part in learning safe driving behaviors before you proceed. It is helpful to have frank and open discussions about the safe behaviors you will expect your teen to demonstrate. If your teen is not able to talk with you about any of the following topics and rules in a respectful and adult manner, delay getting a learner's permit until your teen is able to do so.

1. Prescribed medication for AD/HD and any coexisting disorders will be in effect when the teen is driving if such medication improves the teen's ability to focus and drive safely. Medication schedules may need to be extended to cover driving times.

2. Unacceptable behaviors such as arguing, sassing, and temper tantrums will not be tolerated. These are signs of immaturity and irresponsible behavior. Parents need to make it very clear that driving will not be allowed until these behaviors have been outgrown or are under control.

3. Your teen will start with a learner's permit and gradually earn more driving privileges, based upon successful performance, even if graduated licensing is not the law in your state.

4. The teen will not drive without a learner's permit.

5. The teen driver and all passengers in the vehicle wear seat belts at all times. If your teen neglects or refuses to use seat belts, suspend driving privileges until compliance is assured.

6. Discuss "Good Student" insurance discounts. Insist that your teen maintain schoolwork and grades consistent with (or better than) performance before driving was initiated. Require your teen to maintain schoolwork and grades consistent with performance demonstrated during the time period before driving was initiated.

7. Set a maximum speed limit for beginning drivers.

8. Identify distractions such as music, cell phones, food or other passengers (teens and/or siblings) and spell out your expectations as to how distractions should be handled.

9. Forbid smoking (especially while the teen is driving). With all the information we have about smoking, teens know it is stupid and causes many health problems. For a teenager who is learning how to drive, smoking is also a distraction that can cause crashes!

Illustration by Vicente Utrera

10. Alert the teen to particular safety problems for teens with AD/HD and other high-risk behaviors associated with coexisting disorders.

11. Set expectations for the teen's role in car maintenance.

12. Discuss how to avoid offending and provoking aggressive driving behaviors in other drivers. Talk about how the teen driver can handle personal anger in different driving situations.

13. Discuss road rage situations with the teen and how to behave and disengage from an angry encounter with another driver.

14. Discuss pedestrian safety and a driver's responsibility for pedestrians.

15. Discuss teenage-related auto incidents to understand your teen's view of driving responsibility. Share newspaper articles of teen driving accidents including those resulting in a teen's death. Discuss possible causes of reported fatal crashes. Discuss how the death of your teen driver would impact the family.

Is a Driving Contract Helpful?

Should parents make a driving contract with their teen? Some professionals say that driving contracts can become too restrictive and will undermine the trust between parent and child. Other professionals encourage driving contracts for *all* teens.

Each parent-child relationship is different and parents must decide if the contract would be a helpful tool in managing their teen. Written contracts are adult forms of agreements. Contracts can eliminate power struggles and present rules and expectations for both parties that cannot be forgotten or manipulated. If your teen has difficulty following rules or difficulty following through on agreements, and you sometimes find yourself in arguments or power struggles, the contract can clarify parental expectations. Teens can offer input or suggestions for the contract. However, it is the parent who needs to determine the rules and consequences for poor driving behaviors. Driving contracts can be used to set out your core rules as well as your preventive rules (as described in Chapter 3 of this book) in a clear way that prevents misunderstandings. These rules should clarify your expectations for safe driving behavior and expected consequences if the rules are broken. A standard example of a Learner's Permit Driving Contract follows on pages 93 and 94.

The Teen Driver's Contract for the Learner's Permit

The time to sign agreements about driving responsibility is before the teen is allowed to get the learner's permit and again before application is made for his driver's license. If both parents are going to be involved in the teen's drivers training, they should reach an agreement about the important points in the contract before discussing it with the teenager. Pick uninterrupted family times to talk when you and your teen are in a good mood. Turn off the television and put the phone on hold. Remember to keep conversations with individuals with AD/HD brief, and have numerous discussions to cover all the issues you need to talk about. After the contract is signed, don't stop talking about good driving behavior.

If you decide to use a teen driving contract, it should be written, discussed, and signed by parents and teen. All parties involved must seriously recognize the contract as a binding document. Teens and parents should initial each page of the contract to indicate that all items in the contract are understood. Complex or confusing language should be replaced with simple, understandable language. Both parents and teens should keep a copy of the signed contract. Parents and teens need to agree to rely on the contract to settle disputes regarding behavior and responsibilities.

At his website (www.shiffandpiffle.com) on teen driving, Dale Wisely, Ph.D. advises parents to set a date to review and revise the contract after a designated period of time has passed. Schedule the review date and put it on the family calendar. On the review date, go through the contract with the teenager and make changes as needed.

Better results will be achieved if the contract is customized for each teen rather than using a single contract for all siblings. Family rules and expectations will be the same, but each teen is likely to have different issues requiring attention.

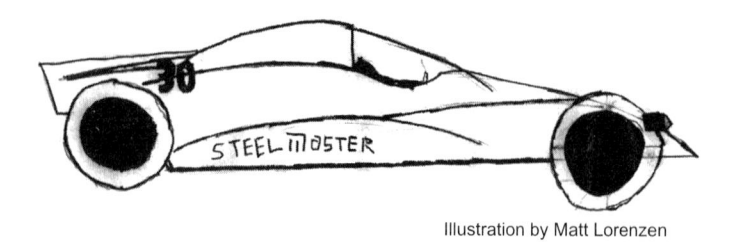

Illustration by Matt Lorenzen

Learner's Permit Driving Contract for:

_____(Teen's Name)

We, the undersigned, recognize that driving an automobile is one of the most hazardous tasks we will undertake during our lifetimes. To help reduce the risks of being a beginning driver, we are entering into this contract. Our goals are to:

1. promote safe driving practices to keep loved ones healthy and alive;
2. operate the family car respectfully and economically; and
3. become responsible individuals within the family and within the community.

It is understood and agreed that having a learner's permit and driving a motor vehicle are privileges extended to teens by their parents. Any privilege has to be earned, and it must be earned on a continuing basis. Your safety is our responsibility and we are taking this action to do what we think is necessary to protect you from harm. We know that sometimes you will see peers who do not have parents who monitor their driving like we do yours. We are your parents, however, and you must abide by our family rules and this contract agreement or you must forfeit your privilege of learning how to drive. We are proud of your accomplishments thus far. We want you to enjoy life and grow up without physical or mental handicaps caused from a motor vehicle crash. If you break the provisions of this contract while you are learning to drive, the consequences will be swift and sure. There is no room for negotiation. Your privilege to drive may be suspended or revoked by Mom or Dad, separately, or together, for any of the following reasons:

1. Failure to comply with directions given during a driving lesson will result in your being instructed to park the car. Your driving privileges will be taken away for the rest of that day. You can try again the next day.

2. You must comply with your medication schedule in order to be allowed to drive.

3. Making mistakes is a part of learning how to drive. Minor learning errors will be pointed out to you. When you make a major mistake, you will be told to park the car. Your driving lesson will be over for that day, and you will have time to think about what you did wrong so that you can learn from your mistake. You will be allowed to try again the next day.

4. If there is any back talk, bickering, or outburst of temper during the time you are learning to drive, it is a sign of immaturity and that you are not emotionally ready to learn to drive. You will lose your driving privileges for a minimum of three days. We will determine when you can try again.

5. Failure to attend school regularly and maintain your school grades, good conduct, and proper attitude at the same high level as when we first granted your driving privileges will result in a loss of driving privileges. A grade of 70 or below in any daily work or test

Initialed: Teen _____   Parent _____   Parent _____

Learner's Permit Driving Contract Continued...

scores in any class will result in the loss of all driving privileges for a minimum of two days. If the poor grade lowers the average class grade below passing, the loss of driving time will be extended until the average for that class is brought up to a passing grade. If you maintain a good school record, you can earn extra driving privileges.

6. Seat belts will always be worn and passengers in the car with you will also wear seat belts at all times. Failure to comply will result in the loss of driving privileges for three days. You can try again in 72 hours.

7. Driving under the influence of alcohol, substances, or inhalants will result in the loss of your driving privileges for 90 days. If it happens twice, driving privileges will be suspended until you have successfully completed treatment.

8. You are never to drive a vehicle that does not belong to us while you are operating with a learner's permit. You may not drive the vehicle of friends or neighbors. You may be allowed to drive with extended family members and drive their cars (such as grandparents, aunts or uncles), but only with our permission before you drive. If this rule is broken, you will lose all driving privileges for two weeks.

9. If the car is taken at any time without an adult, licensed driver, and our knowledge and permission, then driving privileges will be lost for a minimum period of 30 days.

10. If you receive any personal traffic tickets or violation fines while you are driving with the learner's permit, then you will be responsible for paying for them.

11. You will be expected to wash the exterior and clean the interior of the car once a week. Whenever the car is used, we will require that it be returned without any trash or personal items left behind. If trash or personal items in the car become a problem, driving privileges will be suspended immediately. Suspension of driving privileges may be extended for two days after the car has been cleaned.

We have read and agreed with the above rules and the consequences for rule violations. If other circumstances arise that are not addressed in this contract, we agree to handle them through amendments to this contract. Any consequences and additional guidelines shall be written on the back of the contract and will become a part of the contract. We will work together to ensure the safety of all family members in driving.

Signed this _____ day of _____, 20___.

Teen_____

Parent_____

Parent_____

When Contracts Are Broken

Parents need to be prompt, fair, firm, and consistent in monitoring the contract. They must act promptly when there is any violation of contract agreements. Parents should get the facts before taking action, but they should not allow consequences to become negotiable. Manipulative teens can sometimes make their misbehavior seem like they were the victims of an unfortunate situation. Don't allow yourself to fall for this. Violations of contract agreements need to be treated the same way each time they occur.

Parents need to express disappointment when rules are broken. At the same time, they have to act while keeping their anger under control and avoid the escalation of everyone's emotions at difficult times. Parents need to understand clearly that the contract provides for withholding driving privileges, not for withholding love. Both parents and teens will lose when hate or resentment is expressed in their relationship over driving issues.

If your teen refuses to abide by the contract, or argues about agreed-upon consequences, this is a sign of immaturity and a breech of contract. Take the keys and suspend driving privileges until the teen is ready to honor the agreements set out in the contract.

Step #9
Select the vehicle that you will
allow your teen to use while learning to drive.

Select Safe Cars for Teen Driving

The car you choose has great impact on the safety of its driver and passengers. Impulsive teens are usually more concerned about the style, the horsepower, and color of the car they will be driving than the safety aspects of the vehicle. The combination of a high-performance, flashy car and a young, impulsive driver can be very dangerous. The main concern in selecting a car for a new driver should be safety. Think about these things:

1. Because of a higher center of gravity, sport utility vehicles (especially the smaller ones) are less stable than many other vehicles. Through abrupt steering maneuvers, rollovers have caused serious injury and death. Avoid choosing unstable vehicles.

2. Small vehicles usually offer less protection in crashes than larger vehicles. This doesn't mean that you have to buy the largest vehicle that you can find. Many mid- and full-sized cars offer good crash protection.

3. Automatic transmissions are easier to learn to operate, making it easier for your teen to concentrate on driving issues other than shifting gears. If you have to use a standard transmission, begin by giving a lot of extra practice in a safe area such as an unused parking lot. Only after your teen has stopped stalling out, can make smooth shifts without "hopping the car," and can shift while attending to the road, is it time to allow supervised driving of a standard shift vehicle in traffic.

4. Generally, the newer the car, the more safety features you will find. Don't let that statement lead you to think for a moment that you have to provide a new car for your teen to drive! Just look for cars that offer reasonable protection in case of an accident. Most of the cars on the market today are better designed for crash protection than cars manufactured ten years ago. A newer mid-sized car with recent safety features such as air bags and anti-lock brakes would be a better choice than an older, larger car without these features. Look for cars that have a strong safety cage. The safety cage surrounds the compartment where people sit. If the vehicle should roll over, the occupant compartment shouldn't collapse. This is a feature that could save your teen's life!

5. Some vehicles are marketed with a performance image. Sports cars that are marketed as having a big, fast engine are likely to encourage speeding. Choosing a vehicle with a more sedate image reduces the chances your teen will be involved in a speed-related crash. Avoid high-performance cars for new drivers!

6. When you are shopping for a used car for your teen, you may find it enjoyable for both of you to listen to the Tappet Brothers on National Public Radio and to visit their website at www. Cartalk.car.com. Click and Clack often discuss different years and models of cars, and their advice can help you avoid buying a "lemon." You may also call their show to get advice about a

problem that you may be experiencing. They are outspoken advocates for safety, and their humorous presentation of serious issues may be better received by your teen than if you do all the lecturing!

7. If you are purchasing a used car for the teen, take it to an independent mechanic for a comprehensive vehicle assessment. Make sure that all safety equipment is also inspected and in good working order.

8. Check the sales taxes, licensing fees, and insurance rates for the vehicle you are considering before you purchase the vehicle, to be sure that you can afford to own it!

There is a wealth of consumer information available to parents and teens about the safety of cars. One of the easiest ways to find information on auto crash tests is on the Internet. Before purchasing a vehicle, you'll know how much you can afford to spend and what size vehicle you want. Once you've determined the names of vehicles that fit your criteria, you can begin to search for crash-test information for those vehicles.

Crash test studies are conducted annually by the Insurance Institute for Highway Safety and the National Highway Traffic Safety Administration. Parents and teens should take a spin on the information highway and go to www.highwaysafety.org or www.nhtsa.dot.gov. At these sites, you can look up vehicles by their type or model. Compare the safety performance of the vehicle you have chosen with the other vehicles in the same class.

Your insurance company will also have information collected by the Insurance Institute for Highway Safety. This information ranks passenger cars, pickups, and utility vehicles in the categories of injury, collision, and theft losses. It's always wise to consider the safety experiences of others when selecting vehicles for anyone in your family.

Who Should Own the Car the Teen Drives?

Some parents let the teen own a car in order to sidestep higher insurance rates on the family vehicles driven by adults. If the teen has such a high-risk rating that insurance rates skyrocket, should parents continue to let the teen drive? Parents need to consider their answer very carefully. Some parents continue to allow high-risk drivers access to their cars if the teens pay the increased insurance rate. If teen safety is important, however, the car should be parked!

Research from the National Department of Transportation shows that teens who own their own cars have more traffic violations, more motor vehicle accidents, and sustain more injuries than those teens who drive cars owned by their parents. Car-owning teens also tend to earn lower grades in school. Teens who are allowed to buy their own cars usually buy older cars and smaller cars that are not as safe. Allowing the teen to purchase a car may give the message that driving privileges do not have to be earned and that the teen can drive the car at will. When parents retain ownership of the car, they have more control over when, where, and with whom the teen will be driving.

Josh had been given a nice used car so he would have a vehicle to learn how to drive and to provide transportation to school. The very week he received the car, the young man took it out during the middle of the night without permission. While racing with peers, he lost control and drove through ditches before stopping. In the early morning hours, the car was towed to his driveway. Without waking his parents, Josh went back to bed! When his parents awoke, the car was parked in the driveway with long cucumber vine streamers adorning the side mirrors, and a bent axle and frame. Overnight, the wonderful gift had been transformed into a useless wreck.

What Does a Driver Need to Know About a Car?

Teens should be involved in the routine car maintenance. Parents will need to demonstrate the basic maintenance skills to the teen, which include: filling the car with gas, checking the oil, checking air pressure in the tires, filling the windshield washer fluid container, changing a flat tire, and jump starting a dead battery. Teens should be taught to read all gauges on the instrument panel of the vehicle and know what the readings mean. They should also know what to do if they experience problems with the car when their parents are not with them.

General maintenance of a vehicle also includes keeping the car clean — both inside and out! Teens with AD/HD may not stop to consider the appearance of their car and the impression that appearance has on others. Teens need to be taught how to wash a car and do the appropriate detailing on the inside. Parents of teens with AD/HD have often commented about the trash that accumulates in the car. Perhaps this relates to the characteristic of disorganization commonly seen in individuals with AD/HD. For reasons of safety, parents need to stress that unnecessary items in the car be removed.

In an accident, loose items in the car become projectiles. Bottles, CDs, books, shoes, and other items can become dangerous as they continue to travel through the air when the car suddenly stops. Unnecessary objects in the vehicle also constitute distractions to the driver. A trash container should be available for small items. Parents may have to set standards and monitor the general upkeep of the car that the teen is driving.

Periodic Safety Inspections

The Car Care Council suggests a periodic inspection of your vehicle to ensure that everything is working properly. Preventative car care can save time, money, and lives! Occasionally check the function of systems represented on the following checklist, adapted from the Car Care Council.

Comprehensive Vehicle Safety Check	OK	Needs Repair
1. Steering and suspension system, including shocks and struts		
2. Wheel balance and alignment		
3. Braking system, including drums, motors, hydraulics, and electronic components		
4. Emission control system components		
5. Air conditioner, heater, defroster		
6. Speedometer, instruments, and gauges		
7. Lights, horn, mirrors		
8. Windshield wipers and washers		
9. Seat belts		
10. Tires, including spare tire		
11. Fuel system, including computer controls		
12. Ignition system, including computer controls		
13. Battery and electrical system, including alternator output		
14. Cooling system components, including pressure test		
15. Car body (interior, exterior)		

Parent and Teen Activity:

If parents are not skilled in basic car maintenance procedures, the teen and parent may enjoy enrolling in a vehicle maintenance class and learning together. The owner's manual for the car contains a lot of useful information that can be helpful to a driver. It's a good idea to have the teen become familiar with the manual, its location, and the kinds of information that can be found in the manual.

At a minimum, teens should know the following about the car they are driving before applying for the learner's permit:

1. Where the gas gauge is located and how to read it! They should learn how to fuel the vehicle with the appropriate choice of fuel for that vehicle.

2. Where the oil gauge is located and how to read it. They should be shown how to check the amount of oil in the vehicle and the brand and kind of oil that is used in that vehicle.

3. Where fuses are located in the vehicle and how to replace them if needed.

4. How to change a flat tire. Teens should also know if parents have a roadside emergency service plan on the vehicle they are driving and how to access those services. Parents should discuss whether or not they want their teens to attempt to change flat tires on busy highways. Is it safe for a teen to be outside a disabled vehicle in your city or neighborhood?

5. How to "jump start" a car which has a dead battery without causing damage to either the vehicles or themselves!

Monitor Teen Do-It-Yourselfers!

It's not uncommon for teens to want to add a stereo to their cars. Because of the costs of installation, many teens have installed their own stereo systems. If your child is going to do this, be sure that someone who has done this kind of work successfully before assists the teen. Many parents of young drivers can tell you about an impulsive teen who couldn't wait for help and wired a stereo incorrectly, causing a car fire. If you connect a car battery to an amplifier in error, fires are likely to damage the trunk, the back seat, and the roof of the car! Electronically caused car fires often total the vehicle.

A Special Warning — Other Motor Vehicles

Illustration by Harley Addison

When we think about teenagers driving, we usually think about family cars, sport cars, sport-utility vehicles, or pickup trucks. These are just a few of the motor vehicles that teens may have an opportunity to drive. Teens may also have the opportunity to drive or ride motorcycles, boats, jet skis, golf carts, all-terrain vehicles, and snowmobiles. Teens have been seriously injured or killed and have injured and killed others while operating or riding on recreational vehicles.

During 1998, 196 young motorcycle drivers (15-20 years old) were killed and an additional 6,000 were injured. Of these 196 deaths, 53% of the motorcycle drivers were not wearing protective helmets (National Center for Statistics and Analysis). Parents may consider prohibiting teen motorcycle riding on highways altogether, because the death rate on motorcycles is far higher than in cars. Motorcycles require separate training and an additional license to operate them. If teenagers do drive motorcycles, parents should make sure that their teens are equipped with and wear safety helmets and the proper protective clothing.

Other sports vehicles such as boats, jet skis, snowmobiles, and all-terrain vehicles do not require operator licensing because they are not used on highways. We seldom think about the possible injuries and death caused by the inexperienced operators of these vehicles until we read about them in the newspaper or they impact the lives of someone we know.

Teen Drivers of Recreational Vehicles Can Be Criminally Negligent

In the excitement and fun of operating a neighbor's jet ski, a young teen came too close and hit an young female swimmer with the tail end of the jet ski. The swimmer was knocked unconscious and drowned as a result. The 14-year-old was charged and convicted of criminally negligent homicide eight months later.

The driver of the jet ski did not receive appropriate services to help him cope with his emotions after the accident. He became depressed and started running around with teens who drank alcohol and experimented with drugs. After an unsuccessful probation period, he spent three years in a juvenile correction facility. He was never able to make a successful transition back into productive family and community life. Eventually he went from nonviolent law breaking to more serious offenses. The teen is now an adult sentenced to a minimum of seven years in the adult correction system.

In looking over the history of this case, it became clear that the youth had previously been diagnosed with AD/HD, but was taking a "medication vacation" when the accident occurred. (Medication vacations are an outdated practice and are rarely recommended.) Teens with AD/HD need to take their medications regularly, every day — not just when school is in session. Medications are used to help individuals gain control over their behaviors. Medication may not have prevented the accident, but the parents of the teen driving the jet ski and the parents of the dead teenager will forever live with the torment of "what if."

Adolescents with or without AD/HD or other behavior problems should not be allowed to operate any motor vehicles without responsible adult supervision. When teens with AD/HD are operating any motorized vehicle, they should have the benefit of medications that work for them. Parents must take the responsibility of providing the structure and the discipline to see that their teens comply with medication treatment schedules to operate such vehicles as safely as possible.

References:

Car Care Council (2000). *How to Find Your Way Under the Hood and Around the Car.* 42 Park Drive, Port Clinton, OH 43452. Website: www.carcarecouncil.org

Car Talk, National Public Radio. Listen to Click and Clack, the Tappet Brothers and visit their website at www.cartalk.car.com.

Gillis, J. (2000). *The Value Car Book.* New York: Harper Collins.

Gillis, J. (2000). *The Used Car Book: 2000-2001.* New York: Harper Resources.

Shopping for a Safer Car is a brochure that rates vehicle safety on real insurance claims that is available from the Insurance Institute for Highway

Safety by calling 703-247-1500 or visiting their web site at:
www.hwysafety.org

Buying a Safer Car, is a brochure that explains government safety tests.
New Car Safety Features, is a brochure that explains the newest safety
features available. Both of these brochures are available from the National
Highway Traffic Safety Administration. Website: www.nhtsa.dot.gov

Step #10
Make all necessary insurance arrangements.

*"One of the most important tasks parents have before allowing their
teen to drive is to protect the family by purchasing adequate insurance
coverage. Get the coverage and then drive properly so that you never have
to use it." -Dennis Quick, Insurance Agent.*

Select a Reputable Insurance Company

*A good used car was totaled on the freeway because Jennifer had been
following too closely. She rear-ended the car in front of her when that car
suddenly slowed. The driver of the car that was hit indicated that she was
"just fine" at the scene of the accident, but later sued the teen's insurance
company for extended medical costs and damages.*

Select a reputable company and discuss all the possibilities for
adequate coverage with your agent. Discuss all aspects of liability and
collision insurance, considering your total family needs. Issues of insurance
coverage are extremely important and should be discussed thoroughly and
considered very carefully. Every family has to find its own insurance
solutions that reflect careful assessment of the particular insurance circumstances and the teen's driving behaviors. Obtaining ample coverage is of
utmost importance in protecting you and your child from financial liability
for property damage and injuries to others caused by your vehicle. Teens
should never be allowed to drive without adequate insurance coverage.

Many parents don't worry about requiring the teen to repair minor
nicks, scrapes, or dents on their cars, believing that when teens have to live
with visible reminders of minor accidents, they will be more careful. Some
parents may refuse to pay the deductible for these repairs when they have
insured the vehicle in comprehensive policies.

All parents of teenagers, especially parents of teens with AD/HD, need
to consider the addition of an umbrella policy for liability. Be sure that the

liability insurance is adequate to protect family assets in case your teen causes an accident resulting in enormous property or bodily damages. Check the adequacy of your medical health/accident insurance policy as well. Sign up for automatic bank payment of insurance premiums to avoid lapses in insurance coverage because of late payments.

Involve the Teen in Insurance Discussions

Discuss insurance issues and costs at length with your insurance agent with your teen present. Because older cars typically cost less to insure, parents sometimes choose to purchase an older car to be driven by the teen, insuring for liability only. Think carefully about this practice in view of the fact that older cars usually do not have optimal safety features.

When you have purchased your insurance plan, you should schedule a separate meeting between your teen and the insurance agent. It's not unusual for teens to listen to other adults more carefully than they listen to their parents! Ask your agent to explain to your teen how insurance works, the financial benefits that good grades and completion of a drivers education course have on insurance costs, and the consequences of increased insurance costs associated with accidents and traffic violations. The agent may also want to discuss how motor vehicle accidents impact the lives of others by sharing stories about other insured families who have experienced severe injuries and deaths.

Parent and Teen Activity:

Many insurance companies offer videos and other educational packages for both parents and teen drivers. Secure materials from your agent and go through them with your teen, discussing important issues.

Discuss what would happen if your teen's driving led to serious injury or death of any one of your family members or another individual. What services are available in your community to help families cope with the death of loved ones?

Step #11
Apply for the learner's permit only when you and your teen are ready to assume the responsibilities involved.

"By giving permission for our teens to get a learner's permit, we parents are saying that we take responsibly for their driving behaviors."
-Maureen Gill, M.S.W.

Signing the permission slip to allow your teen to secure a learner's permit obligates you to accept financial responsibility for any damage resulting from your teen's operation of a motor vehicle. This permission should not be given lightly, and the implications of this permission should be considered very carefully. Secure the learner's permit only when you are confident that your teen is ready to accept driving responsibilities. If you are using the incentive program suggested earlier in this book, your teen should have earned at least an hour of driving lesson time through the incentive program that you set up.

It's critical that your teen understands that a driver operating a motor vehicle with a learner's permit must have a licensed adult in the vehicle. You may recall from the first chapter that the study conducted in Germany showed many teens with AD/HD had experienced traffic violations **before** they were licensed to drive. Impulsive teens are often tempted to drive without appropriate supervision. Parents always need to control access to the keys. Provide closely supervised driving lessons and plenty of supervised practice driving opportunities. If the teen takes the car without permission, simply withdraw your permission for the teen to drive. The state department of motor vehicles will revoke the learner's permit upon reasonable request from the parent for teens under 18 years of age.

Parent and Teen Activity:
Encourage the teen to take responsibility to find out where to apply for a learner's permit. The teen should call to determine the days and hours that the office is open. Teens should also inquire as to what documentation they need to bring with them to apply for a learner's permit. Some states ask for a Social Security number. Others ask for a birth certificate.
Role-play the process of applying for a learner's permit with the teen.

Step #12
Permit your teenager to sign up for a driver education class at school, but do not abdicate parental responsibility to the school for teaching your teen how to drive safely.

"Hope for the best. Prepare for the worst. Love them no matter what." -Anonymous

Driver Education Classes

Driver education classes should be treated as an excellent supplement to your own driver education efforts. Driver education classes can teach your teen the rules of the road and provide a forum for discussions that will help your child to learn about driving techniques. However, no school driver education program has been able to provide enough behind-the-wheel driver education time to cover all the instruction that a teen needs to become a safe driver. It's unrealistic for parents to expect that teens will learn to be safe drivers with only 3 to 6 hours of behind-the-wheel instruction offered by driver education programs. Unfortunately, schools have cut back or eliminated their driver education programs altogether in many places throughout the country.

If you are one of the lucky parents that has access to a school-sponsored driver education program, take the time to visit with your teen's instructor. Inform the instructor of the teen's strengths and challenges. The instructor should be alerted to any requirements for medications to be in effect while driving, and should be able to schedule your teen's driving experience accordingly.

Parents As Driving Instructors

Sometimes parents worry about not having the skills to teach their teens how to drive. In cases where the parent's driving record is so bad that they are no longer able to hold a driver's license, this worry is well founded. Most parents will make mistakes from time to time, but even though the instruction may be less than perfect, parental instruction may well be the best chance a teen has to learn how to drive safely. The two biggest mistakes parents can make in teaching their teen to drive are discontinuing the instruction process too soon, and turning over to someone else the responsibility for teaching their teen to drive. Parents have the greatest knowledge of how their teen thinks, and they have the most at stake in making sure their teen drives safely.

Before you start the driving lessons, go over the words that you will be using to direct the teen's behavior. State what you expect the teen to do when you give those directions. Be sure you go over the words that you will use when quick and appropriate actions is demanded. Demonstrate for the teen the exact behavior you are expecting when you use these commands. Some of those commands will be:

- Stop
- Slow down and pull over to the side of the road
- Pull over to the curb
- Slow down
- Don't tailgate
- Dim your lights

Don't assume that teens know what to do or how to do it. After you have demonstrated a specific skill, have the teen get behind the wheel and practice the demonstrated skill. Be a coach, not a preacher! Keep teens motivated to learn to become better drivers by providing incentives that they can attain in exchange for good driving performance.

Many parents have found that when they have prepared a lesson and are relaxed, they actually enjoy teaching their teen to drive! In planning the driving lessons, don't try to teach too much at one time. A single concept well taught is much better than a lot of information that isn't learned. Repetition is the key to skill building. Many shorter opportunities to practice basic skills are more helpful than long sessions where the teen becomes overwhelmed with new experiences.

Step #13
Carry out the driving lesson plans you have developed.

"Teach your children to drive as though their lives depended upon it..... because it does."- Parent of a deceased teen driver

States Require Supervised Driving

Many states are requiring a minimum of 50 hours of documented supervised driving instruction before issuing a driver's license. That does not mean that 50 hours is the magical amount of time when all lessons are learned and the license has to be issued. It takes time and a lot of practice to become a safe driver. It's common to underestimate the total amount of time it will take to teach your teen how to drive safely. Most teens will need at least 50 hours, but teens with AD/HD may take three times (150 hours of supervised driving) or longer to master driving skills. Parents should require as many hours as it takes to see the teen become a safe driver before allowing application for a driver's license. Keep a record of the time spent in supervised driving, using a form such as the one that follows. You will want to make at least five copies of the blank form so that you will have plenty of space to record your teen's driving hours. Some states require this log to be presented at the time the teen applies for the driver's license.

Parents Provide Guidelines

Making mistakes is a part of any learning process, including driving. In thinking about how best to facilitate that learning process safely, parents should consider and act upon situations that teen driving research shows to be especially dangerous. Traffic safety experts tell us that safe driving behavior is dependent upon a person's judgment, the amount of driving experience, and the individual's attitude behind the wheel. Because of their age and inexperience, adolescents have not had the opportunity to develop good judgment in driving situations. Adolescents are also at the stage in their lives when they feel invulnerable to physical injuries or death, and they struggle for independence from their parents. This combination often produces a dangerous attitude that results in teens trying out risky behaviors.

Parents can help teens gain experience while reducing risk of vehicle crashes by limiting the situations in which they can drive. Teens need supervised driving time behind the wheel in a variety of traffic conditions, at different times of day, and in challenging weather conditions, before they are ready to drive by themselves. The amount of time you spend in driving lessons with your teen is really up to you, your daily schedules, and your teenager. Learning time can be spent an hour at a time, two or three times a week, over the course of a year, or parents can concentrate the lessons into daily sessions over a half year. Remember that individuals with AD/HD can concentrate for longer periods of time on activities that they are interested in doing. Observe your teen as you are going through the lessons. Lengthen the lesson if your teen is handling the new skills well and is attentive and cooperative. Stop the lesson if you notice fatigue, a loss of interest in the instruction, irritation with the instructor, frustration, or overly confident behavior. Try again when the teen is alert and cooperative.

Patience in teaching the teen driver is essential. Try to remain calm and relaxed during the sessions. If serious driving mistakes are made or your nerves are set on edge, stop the lesson for the day and allow the teen to drive again the next day. It is never helpful to argue with or yell at your teen. When serious driving mistakes are made, you must keep your emotions under control. Simply instruct the teen to pull over, stop the car and change seats with you. Talk over what was wrong with your teen's performance and how the mistakes could have been avoided.

Remember that AD/HD is not a problem of knowing what to do. The problem is with performance — doing what you know! With practice, your teen's performance will improve. Keep practicing until good performance becomes habitual. If parents don't correct bad performance, your teen will not learn safe driving habits.

Parent and Teen Activity:

Share your lesson plans with your teens. Ask them to determine if you have planned for all the driving skills that they will need to learn. Add to your list any suggestions they make that you overlooked.

Talk to your teens about the locations where you will be starting the lessons. Large, empty parking lots or off-season fair grounds are excellent choices. Explain how their driving experiences will be expanded step-by-step as they gain control of the vehicle and your confidence in their skills.

Set up a routine so that there is a predetermined and scheduled time to conduct your lessons.

Illustration by Vicente Utrera

Teen Driving Experience Log

Name: _____

Date	Daytime Hours	Nighttime Hours	Driving Conditions	Total

One Family's Experience

Our son had been making very steady progress in learning how to drive. We were proud of his safe driving abilities and were considering letting him apply for his driver's license. We promised a family celebration of his new skills by taking a trip to our state capitol, which was about 50 miles away. As a part of this special Saturday, our teen was to drive the entire way. This was to be a good opportunity for him to practice his in-town driving, interstate driving, and navigational skills. We had talked about the trip and he had eagerly looked forward to the day for over a week.

He had showered, groomed carefully, and conducted himself in a very adult manner. The early spring day was full of sunshine and promise! It was a wonderful day to be alive! When it came time to go, Dad was given the front passenger seat and Mom was demoted to the back seat. Backing out of a long driveway went perfectly. The acceleration was gradual. The stop at the neighborhood stop sign was done smoothly. The left turn was executed flawlessly. As the car started to accelerate, however, there was a wham-bang-thump that hit the lid of the car trunk!

What on earth? Our teen's head swiveled like an owl's! He was driving down the street with body twisted and attention focused 180 degrees from the oncoming traffic. Dad grabbed the steering wheel and issued the orders. "Turn around and watch where you're going! Keep your eyes on the road!" When the car was again under control, the orders were, "Pull over to the curb and stop!" Our son got out of the car and went back to inspect the trunk where he saw what the trouble had been. The night before the trip, he had rented a movie and was going to return it on the way out of town. The video that was to have been returned was lying in the middle of the street some yards behind the parked car.

As he sheepishly came back to the car, he said, "It was just the video. I had put it on the roof of the car before we left and forget to get it. It's OK." We agreed that leaving a video on top of the car was a mistake that anyone could make, but we disagreed that everything was "OK." When our teen's attention was diverted to looking toward the back of the car while still driving forward, none of us were safe. Those people in oncoming cars weren't safe. Our teen had committed a serious driver error. Even though it was disappointing for everyone, that was the time to learn rather than a time to celebrate safe driving achievement. The family outing was postponed to the next weekend so that our teen could have the time to think about the seriousness of his error. It was time to reflect on how quickly a beautiful day for living could turn into a day for serious injury or death. It was time for our teen to determine how a safe driver would respond to this kind of situation in the future.

Step #14
Evaluate the driving skills of your teen and provide feedback during and after each lesson. Monitor all agreements in the Learner's Permit Contract.

"Encouragement is like premium gas. It helps to take the knocks out of living." -Anonymous

Individuals with AD/HD seem to do better if they know how they are doing as they proceed through a task. Lots of praise helps build confidence. Use short, positive, affirming, and frequent statements when your teen exhibits good driving behaviors, but don't distract your teen from the driving task. Some examples of encouraging words you might use when teaching your teen are:

Way to go	Outstanding performance
Excellent	Well done
You're on your way	You can do it
Good job	Now you've got it
Good for you	You're on top of it now
I like the way you handled that	Great work

Encourage Your Teen

It's important to communicate encouragement when tasks are difficult for your teen. Some examples of encouraging things to say when more practice is needed to develop safe driving skills are:

Hang in there	You're improving
You'll get it, I know	Be persistent - you can do it
Look how far you've come	Let's try again

Don't get discouraged — we'll work on it
What do you think would help you to learn how to do this task?

It's important to be realistic about expectations from beginning drivers. They are going to make mistakes and parents need to point out areas that need improvement. As with disciplining a child, you need to focus most on the behavior or the skill that was done correctly. Don't insult or put down the child personally. Offer constructive criticism and avoid the impulse to lecture. Provide extra support to practice driving tasks that are the most challenging to your teen.

Self-Evaluation

Evaluation is most helpful to learning appropriate behavior when it provides for and encourages self-evaluation. Parents of teens with AD/HD and other difficult behaviors have observed that their children often do not learn easily from their past mistakes. Recent research in AD/HD has shown that individuals with this condition often have difficulty with executive skills. A helpful way to get a teen with AD/HD to learn how to reflect on their activities is to ask them to verbalize what went wrong and how the problem could have been avoided. It is important to watch for realistic understanding of the problem. It is human nature to want to put the blame on someone else when there is a problem, but this is not helpful for teens who are needing to learn safe driving habits. They must take responsibility for their actions!

It is common for some teens with AD/HD to have trouble sequencing events. Even though it is sometimes very frustrating, parents need to help their teen understand the sequence of events and just where something could have been done to avoid the problem. Parents should also ask the teen to verbalize just how they will go about trying to avoid a similar mistake in the future.

Parent and Teen Activity:

A general Driving Skills Checklist follows. Before being allowed to apply for a driver's license, the teen should consistently score in the "Always" section!

If the teen is taking medications for AD/HD or other coexisting disorders, before being allowed to apply for a driver's license, the teen should consistently score in the "Satisfactory" category of any observations made with the charts appearing on pages 82 and 83!

If they do not score consistently well, merely delay the trip to the department of motor vehicles. Poor scores are an indication that your teen needs more supervised practice and instruction.

Driving Skills Checklist

The Student Driver...	Never	Sometimes	Always
1. Knows location of instruments, gauges, and safety devices			
2. Adjusts mirrors and seat properly			
3. Wears safety belts without being reminded			
4. Is attentive to the driving task			
5. Is aware of and checks for traffic before pulling out			
6. Works to maintain a safe following distance			
7. Demonstrates correct hand position on the steering wheel			
8. Demonstrates the "two-second" rule (Can count 1-1,000, 2-1,000" between the time the back of a car in front of you passes a stationary object and the time the front of your car reaches the same spot.)			
9. Thinks about what other drivers are going to do. Is aware of other drivers' blind spots			
10. Checks blind spots before changing lanes			
11. Is aware of tailgaters and knows how to deal with them			
12. Anticipates changing traffic lights			
13. Checks mirrors frequently			
14. Uses horn appropriately			
15. Signals before making turns and lane changes			
16. Checks for traffic in the passing lane before passing another vehicle			
17. Anticipates possible braking situations			
18. Appears relaxed and comfortable while driving			
19. Does not fidget with the radio, CD, or cell phone while driving			
20. Is comfortable driving at night			
21. Uses high and low beams appropriately			
22. Adjusts speed to road, traffic, and weather conditions			
23. Works to maintain a space cushion or buffer zone on all four sides of the car			
24. Checks for oncoming cars when pulling away from the curb			
25. Checks intersections carefully and pauses before entering an intersection			
26. Sets emergency brake or parking brake as necessary before leaving vehicle			
27. Demonstrates smooth movements and good coordination during and after turns			
28. Demonstrates good scanning habits			
29. Obeys traffic laws, including speed limits			
30. Parallel parks skillfully			
31. Backs up accurately and confidently			

Step #15
After basic driving skills have been mastered, expose the teen driver to various driving conditions and prepare for potential driving emergencies.

"Since my kids started driving, my car is insured with Lloyds of Oops!" -Milton Berle

Plan lessons to teach safe driving techniques on wet, snowy, and icy roads, crowded two-lane roads, rural gravel roads, interstate highways, and in various weather conditions including rain, fog, and high winds. Also, plan to teach techniques that help reduce the risk of accidents in night driving.

Discuss the various driving conditions and how to avoid dangerous situations before the teen gets behind the wheel to practice. Explain your expectations as to how your teen should handle the obstacles they may face. For example, talk about the dangers of braking on slick, icy roads and demonstrate appropriate braking techniques **before** you allow the teen to drive on ice! If driving simulators that teach these techniques are available in your area, then teens may benefit from this experience before driving in real weather conditions.

Look up information about how to teach teens about these safety hazards and special weather conditions and plan your driving lessons well. For example, AAA gives the following advice for parents teaching teens about the hazards of winter driving (www.aaa.com/news12/Traffic/yngdrivers.htm).

Winter Driving

For those families living in locations where snow and ice are common, the teen should get ample experience driving in those conditions while licensed with a learner's permit.

- A novice driver's first on-road experience with winter weather driving conditions should not occur during a major blizzard. Wait until conditions are less severe.

- Consider limiting your teen's driving on slippery conditions to daylight hours at first.

- Go to a wide-open snow or ice-covered parking lot. Under close supervision, let your teen practice slow speed maneuvers, including braking hard and steering in skidding situations where there is no chance to hit another car. (Warn your teen about taking a group of kids to "turn 360's" after they are licensed, or being a passenger on such an excursion. Even though it may be "thrilling," skidding on ice and snow can be deadly!)

- Winter weather is tough on a car's mechanical systems, and stopping in slippery conditions requires brakes and tires that are in top condition.

Give frequent feedback to your teen as you go through each lesson. Take time for a longer evaluation at the end of each of your driving sessions.

Prepare Emergency Information and Equipment

Discuss the importance of being prepared with the following information in case of an emergency.

Emergency Information Checklist
1. Vehicle registration
2. Insurance identification card
3. Insurance agent's contact information
4. Emergency phone numbers
5. Parents' home phone number/s
6. Parents' office phone number/s
7. Coins for emergency phone calls
8. Physician's medication letter

Check to see that each vehicle your teen is driving has essential emergency equipment.

Emergency Equipment Checklist	
	1. First aid kit
	2. Flashlight
	3. Blankets
	4. Jumper cables
	If you live in snowy areas you will need:
	5. Sand or non-clumping kitty litter
	6. Small scoop
	7. Ice scraper
	8. Extra windshield cleaning fluid
	9. Other

Teach Appropriate Behavior in Emergency Situations

Role-play emergency situations with your teen before the driver's license is issued. Discuss various situations with your teen and talk about how you expect them to respond in emergency situations.

• What do you do when a fire truck or an ambulance is either in front of or behind you?

• Be sure your teen understands the risks of moving injured persons, how to administer emergency first aid, and the importance of remaining calm and still if injured.

• Assure your teenager that if an emergency should occur, you will be there to help. Make it clear that you expect to be informed of a problem as soon as possible.

Caution Against Hit-and-Run Accidents

Stress the importance of staying at an accident scene. Talk about the basic instinct to flee unpleasant situations and why those involved should stay at the accident scene. Make sure your teen knows that hit-and-run is a crime that can have more serious consequences than the accident itself.

A young lady with AD/HD had an accident at 2 a.m. She was supposed to be home at midnight. Even though she knew she had insurance for the accident, and the problem was relatively minor, she fled the scene. Within an hour, police came to her home and she was arrested. Later she said that she had panicked because of worrying about what her parents would do. Now she realizes that she should have stayed at the scene of the accident. Her parents would have probably punished her for being out beyond her curfew, but their punishment would have been minor compared to the punishment she now faces through the criminal justice system.

Parent and Teen Activity:

Assemble an "Emergency Information Packet" and an "Emergency Equipment Kit" with your teen. Place an identical packet of information in the glove box or a storage compartment of each vehicle your teen may drive. As your teen puts these items from the above checklists into the packet, discuss their importance. Ask your teenager to explain to you exactly what to do in an emergency situation.

Bystander Care for the Injured:
First There, First Care Campaign

Did you know that many people injured in vehicle crashes die before emergency medical technicians can reach them? Many motor vehicle fatalities result from an airway obstruction or the loss of blood that could have been treated by trained bystanders. The first few minutes after an automobile accident are critical. The National Highway Traffic Safety Administration and the Health Resources and Services Administration are launching the First There, First Care Bystander Care Campaign to teach Americans how to provide emergency roadway assistance to the injured until the paramedics or police officers arrive. This education is especially important in rural areas because of the distances first responders must travel to reach the scene of a collision.

Parent and Teen Activity:

Organizing a "First There, First Care: Bystander Care Campaign" could be an excellent project for parents and teens if a program does not exist in your community.

Fax a request to the National Highway Traffic Safety Administration at 202-366-7721 to obtain more information about training packages with public information materials and fact sheets. You may also request materials from their website at www.nhtsa.dot.gov/people/injury/ems.

Step #16
When all instruction and evaluation have been completed satisfactorily, prepare your teen for the driver's license examination.

"Humiliation is not a behavior management technique."
-Clare B. Jones, Ph.D.

Preparing for the Test

Prepare your child for the driver's examination well in advance by talking through the process of filling in forms and taking the vision, written, and driving tests. Talk about appropriate behavior when your teen meets the driver's license examiner and other officials involved in the licensing procedure.

Your teen should practice filling in forms and be reminded that printing the information on the forms is often required rather than cursive writing. Some states require individuals to provide their Social Security number for licensing. Your teen should be prepared with the number at hand. Sample driver's examination tests are located on the internet (Website: www.golocalnet.net/drive/).

Remind your teen to go to the test well rested and well groomed. The teen should be proud of the identification picture that is taken for the new license.

Parent and Teen Activity:

Role-play for your teen the process of introducing yourself to the officials at the Department of Motor Vehicles and how you go about asking to take the driver's license examination.

Locate sample driving tests on the Internet and in driving materials you have accumulated, and administer those exams during your practice session. If you would prefer, make up your own test using information taken from your state's driver's manual. If your teen has difficulty with written tests, practice several different tests over time.

Role-play the driving test. In addition to driving straight ahead, ask your teen to stop at intersections, make both right and left turns into proper lanes, demonstrate appropriate signaling, perform braking procedures, back the car into a specific place, and parallel park. Use the Driving Skills Checklist in Step #14 for additional maneuvers that may be required in the driving test.

Role-play appropriate behavior for success in the driving test. Discuss how your teen should behave if they should fail either the written examination or the driving test. Talk about the words that your teen should use in either situation when communicating with the driver's license examiner.

Step #17
Negotiate a new contract for after
the teen is licensed.

"It is extremely important to think about the consequences of teen driving. Just a moment of carelessness or inattention can cause years of anguish and regret." -Lee Snyder

As you communicate with parents of teenagers who do not have AD/HD, don't be surprised if they question why you are using a driving contract with your teen. They may even tell you that you are being too strict and that you are not developing "trust" in your child. It's not unusual for parents of teens who do not have AD/HD to be critical of the parenting skills of parents of children with AD/HD. Parents of children with AD/HD face this bias over and over again. Just remember that you know your teen better than anyone does. Because of behaviors associated with AD/HD and coexisting disorders, your child has unique needs for guidance, clear rules, monitoring, and consistent administration of appropriate consequences. Never forget that your child's safety is your responsibility!

At this point, your teen is nearly ready to assume the responsibilities of driving the car without adult supervision. When driving with the learner's permit, your teen has always had an adult with them. There will be a few more points that must be discussed and some additional rules established before your teen drives alone. They include:

1. Set strict curfews for both weekdays and weekends.

2. Discuss the limitations on the places and the times of day that the teen can drive.

3. Prohibit the driving of vehicles that are not owned by the teen's parents.

   Even though Kevin had been warned not to drive other people's cars or to allow others to drive his car, he broke both rules. He borrowed a high-performance sports car from an adult friend. While making a turn at an intersection, he ran into the curb, ruining a front axle and costing around a thousand dollars to repair. Police were called to the scene, but the parents of the driver were not. The owner of the car was not insured, so the "borrowing" teen had to pay the repair costs. Less than a year later, when this young man lent his car to a "friend," the driver had an accident involving another vehicle. The teen's friend refused to take responsibility for the repairs, requiring the young man to pay for these repairs as well. Luckily, there were no injuries in either accident. If injuries are involved, legal issues of car ownership become very important.

4. Determine serious consequences for the use of any illegal drugs and alcohol. Enforce no-drinking-and-driving rules.

5. Determine who will pay for gas, insurance premiums, vehicle maintenance, fines for traffic infractions, and vehicle repairs. Teens should be expected to pay for all (or a fair share) of the repairs and expenses when their driving behavior is at fault.

6. Discuss how the death of another person involved in an accident where the teen is driving would impact the life of the teen driver and the families involved.

7. Restrict teen passengers. The best policy is not to allow your teen to drive with other teens as passengers, and don't allow your teen to be a passenger in the car of another teen driver.

8. Require that parents be kept informed of the teen's driving activities.

9. Discuss the location and use of emergency items such as money for phone calls, maps, insurance information, and a list of steps/actions to take if an accident occurs.

10. Address your expectations for the use of the family car. Acknowledge the fact that teens often use parked cars as a private place to experiment with sexual activities. Discuss your expectations for appropriate behavior. Teach abstinence if that is your choice, but at the same time don't ignore the reality of early sexual activity in teens with AD/HD. Research from the Milwaukee Study by Dr. Barkley and others alerts parents that teens with AD/HD are more likely to engage in their first sexual relationship at a younger age than teens without AD/HD (15.4 years of age versus 16.5 years of age). Teens with AD/HD are also more likely than teens without AD/HD to have multiple sexual partners, less likely to use birth control, and more likely to have children before the age of 21. Educate your child about being sexually responsible to avoid an unplanned pregnancy and/or sexually transmitted diseases.

11. Be sure to include incentives and rewards for compliance with the rules and for safe driving behaviors in the contract.

12. Discuss how the death of another person involved in an accident where the teen is driving would impact the life of the teen driver and the families involved.

For teens, Friday night is a good time to be alive! School responsibilities are over for another week and it's time to kick back and have fun with friends! For Chuck, Friday night meant picking up his best buddy, Aaron, to take a couple of girls to a dance and socialize! Christmas holidays were starting the next weekend – everyone was in a festive mood.

Even though they were underage, they purchased some beers from an adult friend to celebrate. Life was good!

Around 1:30 a.m. the two guys delivered a girl to her home and took off across the South Dakota plains. It was cold, windy, and snowing. Aaron was in the passenger seat, unbelted and sleeping when Chuck popped over a hill top and was surprised by a snow drift! Chuck was also unbelted and hung on tight to the steering wheel as he slammed on the brakes and tried to steer clear of danger. Despite all his efforts, his new red pickup truck went out of control and rolled several times into the ditch!

When the truck finally came to a stop, Chuck was stunned. He quickly took inventory of his injuries – just a few minor cuts and bumps! It took a few seconds longer to realize that Aaron was no where in the truck. Chuck searched for his cellular phone, but couldn't find it. He crawled out of the wreck and in the darkness could see the outline of his friend's body laying on the road – yards away from where the truck came to rest.

Chuck made his way to his friend who was laying motionless and bleeding on the frozen, snow covered gravel road. They were half a mile from a major highway. Without the phone, there was no way to call for help. Chuck took off his coat and covered his injured friend and went back through the snow drifts to the crumpled vehicle to look again for the cellular phone. It was no where to be found!

Even though he knew the risks of moving an injured person, especially one with head and neck injuries, Chuck felt that he had no choice. Aaron would freeze to death if he left him there. With each step he took carrying his friend, Chuck was praying for help. As he reached the highway, he could see a set of headlights approaching. He put Aaron down at the side of the road and waved frantically for the motorist to stop. It was a miracle that someone would be driving that early in the morning on that highway!

Chuck's parents were awakened around 4:00 a.m. with a call from the emergency room at the hospital. For a few minutes they were relieved that Chuck was fine, but then learned the news that Aaron was in critical condition. It would be several days before anyone would know the full extent of Aaron's injuries. Chuck failed a breathalizer test and was charged with DUI and minor in possession. He was arrested, handcuffed and taken to a jail cell until bond was posted. He was placed on probation and his driver's license was suspended.

Parent and Teen Activity:

A sample teen Driver's License Contract appears on pages 126 through 129. This sample is especially long because it's a composite of several items that experienced parents have included in contracts with their teens. The contract can be as simple or as involved as you wish to make it. Select those items that are important to you and your teen, disregard the items you don't need, and feel free to add sections to address other important issues.

Step #18
Contact your insurance agent again to be sure the teen is covered when driving with a graduated or unrestricted license.

"It is important to recognize that each time you or your child is in the driver's seat, you are at risk of injury, death, or the loss of financial assets. It is extremely important to communicate with your insurance agent to help reduce your exposure to these risks."
-Tim Murphy, Insurance Agent.

Jason missed a stop sign when his attention was diverted while looking for the turn for a video store. He hit the other driver head-on in the intersection. Jason and his friend were uninjured, but he totaled the car. Three years later, this same teen was involved in another intersection failure to yield accident that caused very serious injuries. Jason will live with the scars, pain, and a metal rod in his leg for the rest of his life. The nearly new totaled motor vehicle was the least of his parents' worries, but caused the teen new financial difficulty when he found out that he owed the difference between the amount of his loan and the amount paid by the insurance company for the totaled vehicle.

Insurance companies often have different coverage rates when the teen begins to drive alone as compared with rates for the student driver. Don't fail to notify your agent when your teenager becomes fully licensed.

Insurance agents would rather get to know your teen under pleasant circumstances than to have to meet them while working out an insurance claim. Meeting with an insurance agent is also an opportunity for teens to demonstrate a mature attitude and a sense of responsibility for their driving.

It is important for both parents and teens to know how your teen driver will impact your car insurance premiums. Take a good look at what your insurance costs are without the teen driver. Then ask your agent to compute the costs of adding the teen to your policy. Let your teen know exactly what you are paying for their privilege of driving. Ask about discounts for completing a drivers education class and about good student discounts. These discounts can be used as an incentive for the teen to accomplish these goals before the learner's permit is obtained.

Then ask your agent to compute the costs for insuring your teen if the teen has:

- one speeding ticket

- one speeding ticket
- two speeding tickets
- a ticket for negligent driving
- a fender-bender accident costing $2,000 to repair
- an accident involving a serious injury
- a couple of speeding tickets and an accident
- a conviction for minor in possession of alcohol
- an arrest for driving while under the influence of alcohol

Parent and Teen Activity:

It's a good idea to have your teen make another appointment with the insurance agent. The teen can inform the agent about the upcoming application for an unrestricted license. This is an opportunity for the teen to establish a positive relationship with the agent and demonstrate maturity.

Talk to your agent about automatic bank payments of your insurance premiums so that coverage is not discontinued because of a forgotten payment.

Driver's License Contract for:

_____(Teen's Name)

Having a driver's license and driving a motor vehicle are privileges extended to you by your parents. With those privileges there are responsibilities:

1. Responsibility to your parents to follow your family rules;
2. Responsibility to yourself to keep a good reputation within the community and to keep yourself physically safe; and
3. Responsibility to others to not injure them or put at risk their safety and welfare.

We know that sometimes you will see peers who do not have parents who monitor their driving like we do yours. This may seem unfair to you. The bottom line is that we are your parents, and you must abide by our family rules and this contract agreement or you must forfeit your driving privileges.

If you break the provisions of this contract, the consequences will be swift and sure. There is no room for negotiation.

Your privilege to drive may be revoked by Mom or Dad, separately, or together, for any of the following reasons:

1. Failure to comply with your prescribed medication schedule. If you cannot be depended upon to comply with your treatment plan, you will lose your driving privileges until you prove to us you can do so.

2. Failure to drive in a safe, attentive manner. Driving a vehicle without seat belt restraints, breaking any driving laws, playing the radio or stereo too loudly, using a cellular phone or pager while driving, using headphones while driving, or abusing a motor vehicle will result in a loss of your driving privileges for two weeks.

3. Failure to maintain your academic grades, conduct, and attitude at the same high level as when we first granted your driving privileges. A poor grade that lowers your average grade to the failure category in any class will result in the loss of your driving privileges until the grade for that class is brought up to a passing grade. (Parents may wish to specify grades depending upon the student's academic capabilities.) Poor conduct or reckless attitude toward driving will result in the loss of your driving privileges for a minimum of two days.

4. Allowing another person to drive a vehicle entrusted to you. You may not lend our vehicle to your friends. If this rule is broken, you will lose all driving privileges for two weeks.

5. Driving a vehicle that belongs to someone else. If this rule is broken, you will lose all driving privileges for two weeks.

6. Giving rides to persons who are not immediate family members. Permission to have passengers will be given by us only when necessary and will be granted on a case-by-case basis.

Initialed: Teen _____ Parent _____ Parent _____

Driver's License Contract Continued...

If you should have passengers without this permission, and we either see you or it is reported to us that you have passengers riding with you, you will lose your driving privileges for 30 days.

7. Being a passenger in the car of another driver (no matter what the driver's age) without permission from us will result in loss of your driving privileges for 30 days.

8. Failure to abide by set curfew times. Curfew time on school nights is 9:00 p.m. On Friday night and Saturday night, your curfew time will be extended to 12:00 p.m. We may also extend curfew times for special events such as school dances, athletic events, and other activities. We will be waiting up for you to return home every night you are out with the car, so you can always call home without fear of waking us. You will lose driving privileges for a minimum of two days if you are five minutes late. If you are more than five minutes late, we will impose a "no driving day" for each minute you are late. For example, if you are one hour late without letting us know where you are, you will not drive for 60 days. The key is to plan ahead and let us know what you are doing, where you are, and whom you are with. Do not speed to get home on time. Call us and tell us where you are. Your phone call telling us you will be late must be made before the curfew time has expired.

9. Failure to keep us informed. If you should experience any trouble while you are driving (accident, harassment from other drivers, problems you don't know how to handle), call home. We will help you in any way that we can. There will be no consequences if you keep us informed.

10. Failure to bring the car home with enough gas to get to work! We will pay for the gas used in our vehicle for all driving done by you as long as we know where you are going and you have our permission. Special trips may be granted when you have earned our trust and proven to us that you are a safe driver. You may be asked to make your own gas purchases from time to time, depending upon the circumstances. Remember that cars need gas to get to the gas station. Try to keep at least a quarter of a tank of gas in the car.

11. Failure to pay parking tickets. Parking ticket fines will be paid for by the driver who "earned" them. Unpaid parking tickets that accrue additional fines will result in the loss of driving privileges until the parking fine and additional late fees are paid.

12. Repeated violations. Any moving vehicle citations will bring immediate consequences (no bargaining as to when the penalties begin). Your first moving vehicle violation will result in the loss of your driving privileges for 30 consecutive days. A second violation will result in the loss of your driving privileges for 60 consecutive days. A third violation will result in the loss of the use of the car for

Initialed: Teen _____ Parent _____ Parent _____

Driver's License Contract Continued...

at least 90 consecutive days, or we may determine that your driving behaviors present too great a danger to yourself and others to allow you to drive. We may withdraw our permission for you to have a driver's license at any time we see fit.

13. Failure to return the car free of trash and your personal items. Whenever the car is used, it is expected that it will be returned without any trash or personal items left behind. If trash or personal items in the car become a problem, we will suspend your driving privileges until the car is cleaned, and we may continue to deny your driving privileges for two days after the car has been cleaned.

14. Failure to park the car in a designated parking area when used for school. When you are allowed to drive the car to school, you will consistently park the car in a designated parking area. This is a family car and may need to be used by another member of the family during the day. These situations will be communicated to you as far in advance as possible, but we reserve the right to pick up the car from the parking area and use it when needed. We will make every effort to return the car to the parking area before school hours are over. Failure to park the car in the designated parking area will result in the loss of the use of the car for school and will result in a further loss of driving privileges for two days. Using the car to skip school will result in the loss of driving privileges for two weeks.

15. Using the car without permission. If the car is taken at any time without our knowledge and permission, your driving privileges will be lost for two weeks.

16. Arguing, back talk, defiant behavior, and attempts at manipulation. Any arguing, back talk, defiant behavior, or attempt at manipulating former agreements about the loss of driving privileges will result in an additional three-day loss of driving time.

We will offer incentives where you may earn special rewards and driving privileges when you exhibit good driving behavior. These extra credit opportunities will be available through your token system. Some opportunities are:

a. Complying with house rules for one week:
additional driving time or additional allowance may
be awarded.

b. Complying with all school rules for five consecutive days:
additional driving time, additional allowance, or special
activity may be awarded.

c. Safe driving for a period of two weeks (14 days)
and compliance with all rules: extra allowance,
additional car use, or extended curfew for a special
event may be awarded.

Initialed: Teen _____   Parent _____   Parent _____

Driver's License Contract Continued...

A good driving record pays. If your safe driving results in relatively low insurance rates and you have had no accidents or traffic tickets for some time, we will reward you.

a. Following 30 days of such safe driving you will
earn _____.

b. Following 180 days of such safe driving you will
earn _____.

c. Following 365 days of such safe driving you will
earn _____.

We have read and agreed with the above expectations and rules. We agree upon all the consequences for rule violations, citations, or vehicle accidents. If other circumstances arise that are not addressed in this contract, we agree to handle them through amendments to this contract. Any consequences and additional guidelines shall be written on the back of the contract and will become a part of the contract. We promise to work together to ensure the safety of all family members.

Signed this _____ day of _____, 20____.

Teen _____

Parent _____

Parent _____

Step #19
When responsible, safe driving behaviors have been demonstrated and good habits have been established, allow your teen to apply for the driver's license.

"Compliance comes from training, background, the fear of getting caught, and understanding that they could be seriously injured or seriously injure another person." -David Turner, M.A.

Do you feel completely safe as a passenger when your teen is driving? Do you cringe at the thought of meeting your teen driving a vehicle in the lane coming toward you? If you do not believe that your teen can operate a vehicle safely, then the teen's license application should be delayed! Permission to take the driver's license examination should only be given when you feel confident in your teen's driving experience, judgment behind the wheel, and attitude toward serious driving responsibilities.

Teens should know that people fail driver's examinations routinely when they do not pay careful attention to the instructions given to them by the examination officers. You should prepare the teen for the possibility of not passing the examination the first time. You may want to role-play appropriate responses to the license examiner if your teen should fail. You may even want to role-play inappropriate responses so that the teen can see how these responses would look to others. Temper tantrums, bad language, or inappropriate behavior or body language are indicators of immaturity. If your teen should display this kind of inappropriate behavior, there would be no question that the examiner did the right thing in denying the driver's license! Provide assurance that if it is necessary, the teen will be given the opportunity to practice driving skills and apply again at a later date.

Illustration by James Pinko

Parent and Teen Activity:

The granting of a driver's license is a memorable lifetime achievement. Parents should accompany the teen to the driver's license examination. Your teen will still be operating under a learner's permit. Allow your teen to drive to the examination. Plan your day so that you will have time to celebrate the successful attainment of the driver's license with your teenager immediately after the license is granted. Let your teen drive to this event as well.

Parents should not allow the newly licensed teen to take off to celebrate the new driver's license with their peers. Sadly, newspaper stories commonly report the death of a teen driver who perished within hours of getting a driver's license. Securing a driver's license is not a reason for irresponsible, unsupervised celebrations.

Also, make a contingency plan for what you and the teen will do if the first attempt at passing the driver's license exam is not successful. Listen to your teen and jointly determine why the attempt was not successful. Identify whether the problem lies with the written test or the driving test. Help your teen identify the specific problem and work on those skill weaknesses so that the next attempt will be successful.

Step #20
After the driver's license has been issued, continue to monitor the teen's driving behaviors, administer consequences as needed, and insist that all contract agreements be honored.

"Take on your problems one by one and work things out."
-Bruce Steadman

Parents need to remember that once the teen gets the license, their responsibility as parents does not end. In fact, this is the very time that parents need to be most vigilant! The first year of driving is a high-risk period for the beginner. Inexperience combined with a lack of skill means that on average, one in five male 16-year old drivers and about one in ten females will have an accident during their first year of driving.

Continue to monitor your teen's driving behaviors closely. Watch for the accumulation of bad habits such as forgetting to signal, sloppy turns, speeding, changes in speed or direction, or lack of alertness. Continue to invest time and energy in more education and practice time to improve driving behaviors.

My daughter has AD/HD. She has had her driving license less than a year and has had five accidents. The last one was a collision with a school bus. What can we do to help her become a better driver? (Adapted from an article written by Bob Seay, add.about.com)

Bob's answer included the following:

"My first recommendation for your daughter would be to take away her keys before she gets seriously hurt or kills somebody! ...... Your daughter may not like losing her driving privileges, but unless she gets this under control, she will end up dead. I've buried more students than I care to remember. Almost every one of them had survived several accidents before the eventual tragedy that took their lives. In fact, it sometimes seems that surviving an accident only reinforced the idea that they were not going to get hurt. You and I both know that it's only a matter of time."

Teens must understand that they need to continue to earn the privilege to drive. Usually teens do very well immediately after their license is issued, but after they have had their license for a few months, it's common for them to start ignoring safety rules and begin taking more risks. Parents need to be able to resist pressure from their teens to make exceptions to rules. The novice driver's biggest enemy is the complacency that comes from early success in learning driving basics. The parents' role is to help their teens overcome that complacency and continue to build driving skills after licensing.

Nathan got two speeding tickets within the first six months after getting his driver's license. His insurance rates zoomed from $40 to over $300 per month. Instead of focusing on paying the high cost of insurance, his parents focused on Nathan's safety. His car was sold and Nathan is relying on other forms of transportation!

If the teen respects the rules and demonstrates responsible driving behaviors, be sure to provide rewards. These rewards may be in the form of more driving time, extending a curfew for a special occasion, or driving for a special family event. Ask your teen to identify important personal incentives. One of the strongest motivators is parental approval. Take the time to tell your teens sincerely and often that you are proud of them when you see them demonstrating responsibility in their driving behaviors.

Cars and College

Many teens with AD/HD enroll in technical school or college after their high school graduation. Sometimes having too many new experiences at one time causes difficulties for teens. Experienced parents will tell you that, if at all possible, it is best not to complicate the teen's adjustment to college life by having a car at their disposal

Once teens with AD/HD are away from the structure of living at home, many have difficulty remembering to take their medications. They lose focus on their educational goals. Having a vehicle available to them is an irresistible distraction. In their interest to go places with friends, they neglect their studies and classes. Many fall hopelessly behind in their school work, become discouraged, and drop out of school.

Many parents have found that students with AD/HD do better without cars on campus during their first year in post-secondary education. These teens can be required to earn the privilege of having a car at school by first showing parents that they can handle their educational courses.

Resources:

Bob Seay is the About.com guide on AD/HD. His website provides breaking news, research information, and discussions about AD/HD.
Website: www.add.about.com/health/add

Chapter 5

Handling Poor Driving Behaviors

"It was fun, fun, fun ... 'til her daddy took the T-Bird away!"
-Beach Boys

It is the parents' right and responsibility to suspend and restore their teen's driving privileges, even after their child is fully licensed. Parental control of the keys underscores the fact that driving is a privilege — not a right. Parents should continue to monitor the teen's driving behaviors and take action, if necessary, before serious driving infractions occur. Consequences have previously been agreed to in the driving contract and should not come as a surprise to the teen! Don't relent or try to protect the teen from unpleasantness. Keeping any teen driver safe is hard work. The additional difficulty caused by characteristic AD/HD behaviors makes this task even harder!

If parents observe poor driving behaviors along with defiance or aggression, they should take away the keys, the teen's license, and all driving privileges until self-control has returned. It's sometimes very hard to do this. Many parents have caved in to demanding teens. This does nothing but teach the teen that they can get away with anything — including disrespecting their parents. Legally, the license and the keys belong to the parent while the teen is a minor. It's possible and prudent for parents to withdraw permission for the minor's driver's license at the state's department of motor vehicles if the teen's driving behaviors are unsafe and their attitude is uncooperative. Parents need to take control of the situation and, when necessary, seek professional help if serious behavior problems arise.

You may find it helpful to invite friends and neighbors to comment on their observations of your teen's driving behaviors. Both positive and negative comments are important. Some parents have found it helpful to use a teen driver monitoring service (as described in Chapter 4) to minimize poor driving behaviors.

When Violations Occur

When a contract violation occurs, express your concerns for your teen's safety. Let your teen know that there is no problem that your family cannot get through. Resist the temptation to say, "I knew this would happen" or "I told you so." Listen to your teen's perceptions of what happened; then refer to the written contract and follow the agreement. Calmly and immediately administer consequences without anger. Agreed upon consequences are nonnegotiable! It is especially important to follow the consequences the first time there is a problem. If parents do not act confidently, teens quickly learn that the agreement is not important. Parents then open themselves up to having their teen question all rules, and threatened consequences become meaningless.

Don't be afraid to restrict or remove driving privileges as needed. As the parents, you must be in control in order to teach your teen drivers that they are responsible for their driving behavior. Teens may need to be reminded that all accidents are preventable. They should not be allowed to think that everything that goes wrong with their driving is someone else's fault. Mistakes are valuable only when you learn from them.

Parents need to verbally remind the teen that even though they are withholding driving privileges, they are not withholding their love. It's because parents love their children that they will do everything they need to do (including experiencing the teen's anger) to protect the safety of the teen and others.

Prepare the Teen to Perform Well When Violations Occur

Illustration by Adam McCafferty

Role-play situations to teach how your teen will be expected to behave if stopped by law enforcement officials for a traffic violation. Stress the importance of stopping at the first moment you notice that you are being followed and signaled to pull over by law enforcement officers. Charges can be pressed against a teen for trying to evade a police officer. Depending upon the circumstances, the driver could wind up in jail for not stopping. Have the teen provide the driver's license (taken out of the billfold), the registration papers for the ownership of the car, and proof of insurance. It's good to be sure that the teen is able to recognize each of these documents and knows how to present them when requested to do so. Teens must understand how showing disrespect toward a law enforcement officer will work against them.

Robert had just graduated from high school in May and was attending a rural community carnival. While traveling on a gravel road, he was speeding. He saw the lights from a police car flashing, knew he was in trouble, but tried to outrun the police officer. He lost control of his vehicle on the gravel road. It rolled several times before coming to rest. Sadly, Robert, who had a promising future, was killed in the crash.

Parent and Teen Activity:

If possible, allow your teen to participate in a local law enforcement "ride along" program. Observing traffic violations first hand, from the perspective of law enforcement officials, can be a more effective way to learn than listening to parents. Read traffic court news and visit a traffic court with your teen. Talk about the embarrassment of having the teen's name in the newspaper and/or having to appear in court.

Selecting an Attorney

There are occasions when consulting an attorney may be in the best interest of your teen driver. One such occasion is when the teen is involved in a personal injury accident. Another is if the teen is accused of committing a crime while using your vehicle. The teen should consult with an attorney before admitting guilt for driving violation charges. Do not let your teenager go to court without competent representation when facing serious charges, especially in those cases involving personal injury accidents. The following items are important for parents to consider when selecting an attorney to represent their teen when charged with a serious driving offense.

- Is the attorney willing to learn about AD/HD and how it impacts your teen's behavior?

- What have been the outcomes of similar cases that this attorney has defended, especially those cases involving AD/HD?

• What is your court's view of cases involving teens with AD/HD?

If you need to select an attorney and have no idea where to begin, it might be good to start with inquiries to friends. Other parents in a local Children and Adults with Attention Deficit Disorders (CHADD) chapter, or other parent support groups, may have already had a similar experience and know of a good, local attorney. Another suggestion is to contact your local library for a list of defense attorneys practicing in your area.

Can AD/HD Be Used As a Legal Defense?

The diagnosis of AD/HD does not excuse inappropriate driving behavior and should not be used as a defense. If AD/HD characteristics contributed to unsafe driving behavior, this information may be offered to the officials of the court in order to provide a better understanding of the teen. Officials of the court can use information about AD/HD in the adjudication process to develop more meaningful consequences for the teen. Requiring appropriate treatment programs, extended time on the learner's permit, or medication compliance during driving times may be called for in an effort to help prevent the same mistakes from being made again. It is the responsibility of the court, as well as the parent and the teen, to insure the safety of the community.

Parents should inform their attorney of their teen's AD/HD diagnosis, and the attorney in turn will inform the court. Discuss possible consequences with your attorney and look for fairness in determining consequences from the court. If parents have suggestions for reasonable consequences, penalties, or treatments, present them to the attorney. If families have possible solutions that will satisfy the court, these solutions are often heard in court and taken into consideration in the adjudication process.

Parents should also inform the attorney of any learning disability that might impact the teen's ability to answer questions in the courtroom environment. When testifying in court, for example, some teens with AD/HD have a difficult time sequencing events. They may tell the story in several different ways or confuse the times. This may give court professionals the impression that the teen is lying. Attorneys and judges need to be alerted to the teen's difficulty with this aspect of language skills. Under the Americans with Disabilities Act, teens may be able to receive accommodations in the courtroom that will allow for their disabilities. For example, teens with AD/HD who have difficulty with language processing can be given more time to answer questions, submit written statements detailing events, or they may need to have all questions offered in simple terms they can comprehend. "Legalese" should not be used without careful explanation and the certainty that the teen truly understands what is happening.

Professionals involved in law enforcement or the justice system may or may not know about AD/HD. Judges and probation/parole officers, law enforcement officers, and others may find educational materials at the Children and Adults with Attention Deficit Disorders website (www.chadd.org). Technical assistance and training regarding AD/HD for professionals working in the juvenile justice system are available from the National Council of Juvenile and Family Court Judges, P. O. Box 8970, Reno, Nevada, 89507 (www.ncjfcj.unr.edu); or from Whitefish Consultants, P. O. Box 1744, Whitefish, Montana, 59937 (www.whitefishconsultants.com).

Expectations of Teens in Court

Parents should always impart to their teens respect for the justice system, and for the professionals working in the court. If the teen is disrespectful and uses swear words, is poorly groomed, dressed inappropriately, or seems disinterested or resistant to the court proceedings, then fines and penalties may be more punitive. The teen should be able to articulate the relevant events in a respectful manner when asked to do so.

Role-play a court situation with the teen before any court appearance. Eye contact, neat personal appearance, and body language are important to discuss and demonstrate. Practice appropriate verbal and body language responses, as defendants need to present themselves well. The teen needs to demonstrate respect for the court and accept responsibility for personal behavior.

Forgetting to appear or being late for court can cause further trouble for the teen. Not appearing in court when ordered to do so is a very serious matter in itself and can result in incarceration and/or being forced to post a bond. Be sure the court date is displayed prominently on the family calendar. Parents need to accept the responsibility of taking the teen to the court appearance. Teenagers with AD/HD should never go into a court situation without a caring, supportive adult to help them through the process. Finally, teens should be prepared to follow the judgment of the court and work cooperatively with court officials.

Court Appearances

Parents should not wait for court-imposed fines and penalties to be assessed to teach the teen about the seriousness of bad driving behaviors. Court dates for moving violations usually occur a month or more after the driving offense, however teens with AD/HD need to experience consequences immediately if the consequences are to be linked to their inappropriate behaviors. Delayed court appearances allow teens with AD/HD time to make excuses for the problem and justify their actions in their own minds. The teen's focus may become centered upon their perception of unfairness or upon punitive individuals within the judicial system instead of focusing upon their mistakes. To protect their teen and the community, parents should initiate consequences for poor driving performance and driving contract violations immediately! Consequences administered by a judge should be understood to be in addition to consequences administered by parents.

The experience of being required to appear in court or to enroll in a diversion program is a logical consequence of poor driving behaviors. Parents should check out pretrial diversion programs that may be available to their teens. Participating in such a program will reinforce your teaching points and will help keep insurance costs lower. Check with your local police or county sheriff department or your local court to determine if such a program is available and how to access it.

Court appearances are often inconvenient experiences and produce uncomfortable feelings of guilt or shame. This is a consequence that can teach teens a great deal about taking responsibility for their actions. Parents should not try to soften this experience for the teen. If diversion programs, such as a special weekend driving course, are offered to the teen in lieu of a fine, to save license points or to avoid insurance premium increases, then the teen should be required to take and complete the course.

The teen should be responsible for paying associated legal fees, fines, and court costs that result from driving mistakes. This is also a natural consequence for unsafe driving behavior. Parents should require the teen to be responsible for payment for repairs or increases in insurance premiums when the behavior of the teen causes these additional costs for the family. If absolutely necessary, parents may loan money to the teen to pay for such costs, but driving privileges should be suspended and not restored until the loan is repaid in full. If the fines, repairs, and other expenses become too great for the teen to pay, then the teen should not be allowed to drive. The ultimate natural consequence of a poor driving record is not being able to afford to drive. Parents should feel no obligation to underwrite expenses for an unsafe driver! Keeping an unsafe teen driver off the road is the parent's responsibility.

Parents must monitor their teen's compliance with and satisfactory completion of all court orders. The court experience provides a forum for learning and an opportunity for parents and teens to revisit topics such as appropriate behavior, self-respect, and community responsibility. Parents should express their disappointment in the teen's driving behaviors and reteach the lessons needed to improve driving skills. Parents should be careful, however, not to withdraw their love and emotional support for their teen throughout the court process.

Driving When the License Has Been Suspended/Revoked

In the past, drivers suspended from driving by the court for alcohol-related convictions, failing to pay tickets, or failing to appear in court did not receive additional punishment for driving with a suspended license. This has changed. Now, drivers receive additional sanctions for driving with a suspended license. More importantly, new repeat-offender laws established in some states have created new crimes that include "Allowing Another Person to Drive While Suspended."

People (including parents) who allow a repeat offender to drive their vehicle or who jointly own a vehicle with a repeat offender can be affected by the new repeat-offender laws. If you own or jointly own a vehicle that is used to commit a repeat-offender offense, then that vehicle is subject to immobilization or forfeiture by court order. If a repeat offender drives your vehicle and that person seriously injures or kills another, you may be charged with a two or five-year felony, respectively. State laws also prohibit the transfer of vehicle ownership to avoid immobilization or forfeiture. In short, the message is clear. **Don't let a repeat offender drive your vehicle!**

Organ Donor Authorization

Anyone under the age of 18 may participate in the donation of their tissue or organs through the state organ donor registry with the consent of a parent or legal guardian. If a teen should die in a car crash, parents will be asked if they wish to donate organs to extend or save the life of another person. Having discussed this issue with your teen and having made that decision at the time that the driver's permit is secured can spare families from having to guess the wishes of their teen. Having this discussion before licensure also helps to communicate the seriousness of the teen's driving behaviors.

Parent and Teen Activity:

Have you thought about organ donation in the event that you or a loved one are killed in a car crash? Share your decision about organ or tissue donation with your family now. A simple family conversation will prevent confusion or uncertainty about your wishes. Knowing that they fulfilled your wish to save other lives can provide your family with great comfort in their time of grief. Many parents have found comfort in knowing that when their own child could not be saved, their child's organ's were used to help another person. Contact the Donor Awareness Council at www.donor-awareness.or/driverlic.htm for a family notification form and more information.

The Bottom Line is Parental Responsibility

All parents struggle with challenging issues when their teenage children begin to drive, but for the parents of teens with AD/HD, there are additional issues that must be carefully considered. The best time to think about your responsibilities as a parent is **before** your child is ever allowed to get behind the wheel. If your state does not impose common sense graduated licensing requirements, there is no reason you should not impose your own graduated licensing system. Once your teen begins driving, you should continually monitor, coach, and praise positive driving behaviors and attitudes. At the same time, you must also be vigilant, as well as ready, willing, and able to immediately impose appropriate consequences for rule violations and unsafe driving behaviors. It is your responsibility to protect your teen, other drivers in the community, and yourself!

As a parent of a teen with AD/HD or other coexisting disorders, you will face many challenges that parents of teens without these disorders do not. May you experience good things in life: the happiness of realizing your dreams, the joy of feeling worthwhile, and the satisfaction of knowing that you have succeeded in helping your child develop safe driving habits that will serve them well all their lives. Good luck!

Share Your Story

Hopefully the information presented in this book has helped you to determine how to help your teen with AD/HD to become a safe driver. If you have questions or comments about the materials presented in this book, you may contact the author at: www.whitefishconsultants.com. As the author of this book, and a researcher, I would be interested in hearing your stories about how you used this book and in hearing of techniques that you have used to help your teens with AD/HD become safe drivers.

Index

M

Magnetic Resonance Imaging (MRI), 9, 10
Major depression, 21-23
Manic-depressive disorder, 22
Maturity, 6, 45, 55-58
Mayo Clinic Research, 5
Medications for AD/HD, 19, 45, 49, 52, 54, 61, 74-81
    Effects of, on brain, 12, 13
    Concerns, 16, 76
    Facts and fiction, 75
    Keychains, 80
    Letter from physician, 85
Modeling behavior, 45-48
Monitoring during driving, 46
Mood stabilizers, 77, 78
    Stimulants, 77, 78
    Timing of, 78
    Tricyclic antidepressants, 77, 78
    Types of, 77, 78
    Methylphenidate (Ritalin, Metadate, Concerta), 77, 78
Mood disorders, 21, 22, 23
Monitoring,
    Parental, 6, 38, 39, 40
    Technology for, 39
    Teen monitoring services, 38-40
Motorcycles, 101
Murphy, Kevin, iii, x, 48

N

National Center for Statistics and Analysis, 7, 101
National Council of Juvenile and Family Court Judges, 139
National Highway Traffic Safety Administration (NHTSA), 4, 7, 62, 97, 103, 118, 119
National Information Center for Children and Youth with Disabilities, 31
National Institutes of Health, 16
Neurotransmitters, 12, 13
New England Journal of Medicine, 11, 65, 70
Norpramine (Desipramine), 77, 78

O

Obsessive-compulsive disorder, 24
Observation forms for driving, 82, 83
Organ donation, 141, 142
Operation Lifesaver, 72, 73, 74
Oppositional defiant disorder, 17, 19, 28
Owner's Manual, 100

P

PACER Center, 31
Panic attacks, 23, 24
Parents, vii, ix, 6
Parent expectations for teen drivers, 29
Parent – Teen activities, 28, 52, 62, 67, 73, 80, 84, 100, 104, 105, 113, 118, 119, 120, 123, 125, 131, 137, 142
Parents as driving teachers or coaches, 46, 48, 106
Parents as role models, 46, 47, 48
Parents with AD/HD, 47, 48
Parental monitoring, 38-40
Parental responsibility, 6
Parenting with Dignity, 42, 43
Parker, Harvey, 31, 42, 43, 54, 77, 78, 86, 87, 89
Passengers, 60, 61
Paxil, 77, 78
Pemoline, 77, 78
PET Scan, 9, 11
Praise (see encouragement)
Property damage, 1, 20, 103, 104, 125
Punishment, 41, 42, 53, 118

Q

Quensel, Warren, 57, 58, 71, 74

R

Railroad Crossing Safety, 72, 73
Repeat offenders, 141
Resources, 7, 29-31, 44, 48, 54, 55, 58, 70, 86, 102, 103, 133
Rewards, 87, 88, 122, 132
Ritalin, 76, 77, 78
Road Rage, 49, 52, 91
Rouse, Gerald E., iii, 58